# A
# Roman
# Catholic
# Theology
# of
# Pastoral Care

THEOLOGY AND PASTORAL CARE SERIES

edited by
Don S. Browning

*Life Cycle Theory and Pastoral Care*
by Donald Capps

*Religious Ethics and Pastoral Care*
by Don S. Browning

*A Roman Catholic Theology of Pastoral Care*
by Regis A. Duffy, O.F.M.

**REGIS A. DUFFY, O.F.M.**

# A
# Roman
# Catholic
# Theology
# of
# Pastoral Care

Don S. Browning, *editor*

THEOLOGY AND PASTORAL CARE

**FORTRESS PRESS**
PHILADELPHIA

---

**Library of Congress Cataloging in Publication Data**

Duffy, Regis A.
   A Roman Catholic theology of pastoral care.

   (Theology and pastoral care series)
   Includes bibliographical references.
   1. Pastoral theology—Catholic Church.  2. Catholic Church—Doctrines.  I. Title.  II. Series.
BX1913.D82  1983    253    83–48006
ISBN 0–8006–1727–4 (pbk.)

---

K115E82   Printed in the United States of America   1–1727

# Contents

# Series Foreword

Our purpose in the Theology and Pastoral Care Series is to present ministers and church leaders with a series of readable books that will (1) retrieve the theological and ethical foundations of the Judeo-Christian tradition for pastoral care, (2) develop lines of communication between pastoral theology and the other disciplines of theology, (3) create an ecumenical dialogue on pastoral care, and (4) do this in such a way as to affirm, yet go beyond, the recent preoccupation of pastoral care with secular psychotherapy and the other social sciences.

The books in this series are written by authors who are well acquainted with psychology, psychotherapy, and the other social sciences. All of the authors affirm the importance of these disciplines for modern societies and for ministry in particular, but they see them also as potentially destructive of human values unless they are guided in their practical application by tested religious and ethical traditions. But to retrieve the best of the Judeo-Christian tradition for the church's care and counseling is a challenging intellectual task—a task to which few writers in the area of pastoral care have attended with sufficient thoroughness. This series addresses that task out of a broad ecumenical stance, with all of the authors taking an ecumenical approach to theology. Besides a vigorous investigation of Protestant resources, there are specific treatments of pastoral care in Judaism and Catholicism.

We hope that the series will help ministers and church leaders view afresh the theological and ethical foundations of care and counseling. All of the books have a practical dimension, but even more important than that, they help us see care and counseling differently. Compared with writings of the last thirty years in this field, some of the books will seem startlingly different. They will need to be read and pondered with care. But I have little doubt that the series will make a profound and lasting impact upon the way we understand and practice our care for one another.

Father Regis Duffy writes *A Roman Catholic Theology of Pastoral Care* out of his richly varied educational and pastoral experiences in both France and the United States. After receiving a doctorate at the Institut Catholique in Paris and serving in various pastorates in France, he returned to the United States and soon was invited to teach at the Washington Theological Union. In addition to teaching and doing research, he has continued to serve on the pastoral staffs of various churches in the Washington area.

In this book Father Duffy develops a spirited argument for a reconstruction of the church's practices of pastoral care around the model of the catechumenate. The catechumenate was a challenging ancient process for the formation of candidates wishing to be Christians. It entailed a lengthy process of study and service prior to a final act of baptism. Father Duffy believes that this long process, much of which was built around pastoral service to the needy, the poor, the aged, and others, had a rejuvenating effect on the entire church and taught to both the initiates and the baptized a praxis model of the church and pastoral care. Father Duffy believes this model can be retrieved and he recommends it as a new image of care for both Roman Catholic and Protestant churches.

The catechumenate model is extended by enriching it with another ancient symbol, that of the minister as *medicus* or "doctor of the soul." Father Duffy attempts to reclaim this ancient image of healing, applying it not only to the healing of the body but also to the healing of the soul as a way to both deepen the care of the church and save it from the more juridical and professional models of care that have afflicted not only Roman Catholic pastoral care but Protestant pastoral care as well.

Father Duffy's book presents a powerful summary of the history of pastoral care and retrieves some of its central images and practices. It will go far to create a broadly appealing new ecumenical model for the care of souls in our time.

DON S. BROWNING

# Introduction

Georges Bernanos, the contemporary French novelist, created a sensation some years ago with *The Diary of a Country Priest,* in which he described the vagaries of pastoral care in twentieth-century France.[1] He argued, in effect, that pastoral care is sometimes ineffectual because Christians not only fail to care for one another but even destroy the very people who try to minister to them.

Bernanos's insight, while not new, needs to be repeated with even greater urgency now as the century approaches its close. The books of theology that we write today and the church buildings that we presently construct will one day be what the *Didache* and the house-church of Dura-Europas have become for us—interesting relics of the theory and praxis of Christian communities long gone. But it was the pastoral care of their communities that shaped and influenced the lives of the Christians within them. And it was the pastoral care that these anonymous Christians experienced and shared that made Christ and his gospel realities for them. Pastoral care must do the same for us and our contemporaries.

Within a series of books on the theology of pastoral care that attends to the viewpoints of various Christian traditions, it is important to pinpoint a particularly Roman Catholic development—the gradual clericalization of the care of souls. Heinz Schuster characterizes the culmination of this historical development:

> In the end, the individual clergyman was defined as the historical continuation of the person and function of Christ ("Christ's representative," "God's viceroy," "channel of all graces," "shepherd of the flock," etc.). And the individual Christians and the church congregation stood before him passively, as something "directed," "led," and indeed "sanctified" by him.[2]

In the first two chapters of this book I hope to set this problem in historical context. Chapter 1, "Pastoral Care in the Post–Vatican II

Church," will suggest theological reasons for some of the ambiguities in the theory and praxis of pastoral care. Here the key issues are seen to be not ordination or even jurisdiction, but rather the operative definitions of salvation and the underlying assumptions about the nature and mission of an ecclesial community. Chapter 2, "Pre–Vatican II Theologies of Pastoral Care," will trace certain trends within the history of the Roman Catholic church that illustrate how our current definitions of salvation, church, and pastoral care were derived.

Chapter 3 moves in a rather different direction when it speaks of "The *Medicus* Symbol of Pastoral Care." The metaphor of Jesus as *medicus* or doctor, which bridges the patristic and tridentine understandings of care, is still seminal for any subsequent theology of pastoral care.

Chapter 4 considers the relation of "Praxis and Theology in Pastoral Care." In the current American scene, a split between pastoral theory and praxis is not rare. There is still a good deal of nineteenth-century theory and praxis behind much pastoral care, even though some of the ministerial staff were trained in the post–Vatican II period. To address this problem, some of the insights derived from social-critical theory will be used to reexamine the relation between the mission of the ecclesial community and pastoral care.

In chapter 5, "Theological Issues in Pastoral Care," specific areas of concern in pastoral care, such as education for pastoral care ministries, will be discussed. Of itself, professionalism cannot deal with the theological issues addressed in the first four chapters. Team ministry provides a pastoral model that can make concrete certain otherwise abstract theological concerns.

In the final chapter, "Pastoral Care for Tomorrow," we will look into the catechumenal model for guidelines that might both clarify and critique the pastoral care task. These guidelines will be tested against three pastoral concerns—the sick, youth, and the elderly.

In brief then the principal objective of this book is to situate pastoral care within the mission of the Christian community. This approach does not deny the redemptive needs of the individual, but suggests rather that we can attend to these needs and meet the many demands made upon pastoral care only when we evoke gospel commitment from the people for whom we care.

This theological focus is in no way intended to disparage recent fruitful developments in the psychosocial dimensions of pastoral care. One of the major contributions of twentieth-century pastoral care, for example, is the appreciation of the crucial role of psycho-logical models and insights for clarifying the pastoral situation of both the Christian community and Christian individuals. Sociologi-cal analysis has helped the Christian churches to grasp the larger social dimensions of radical evil and to address neglected issues of justice. The overriding theological concerns of this book assume and employ these contributions of the human sciences.

The basic argument of the book can be stated in this way: Com-mitment to gospel tasks and responsibilities is a key factor in effec-tive pastoral care. We are healed for the sake of others. The praxis of the community and its individual members must be honestly evalu-ated in terms of this gospel perspective. Such an evaluation allows for examining anew the priorities of ministry and pastoral care. Basic questions emerge from such a review: What type of education is necessary for effective pastoral care? Are current models of pasto-ral care based on privatized notions of redemption? What commit-ment should one expect to flow from some of the traditional methods of pastoral care, such as hospital ministry, spiritual direc-tion and counseling, and the sacrament of reconciliation? How does mission, as a frame of reference for pastoral care, expand the moral dimension of such care?

Readers from other Christian communities may find it useful to study the pastoral care theology of the Roman Catholic community. Part of the enrichment that ecumenical dialogue has brought with it in our time is a new awareness of our shared traditions of pastoral care, and of the prophetic challenge that our differences suggest. On the other hand, there would be little value to a theoretical consensus in ecumenical dialogue if the unexamined praxis theologies of our pastoral care traditions were, in fact, deeply divergent.

CHAPTER 1

# Pastoral Care
# in the
# Post–Vatican II Church

Pastoral care is an abstract term that attempts to capture the concrete situations of God's action among us. Pastoral care spells out the real-life implications of that evocative phrase in the opening chapter of the Fourth Gospel: he "made his dwelling among us" (John 1:14). We cannot discuss theologies of pastoral care apart from the situations in which they occur—the enfleshed events of our shared lives where God's mystery of salvation is revealed.

## THE FOCUS ON PRAXIS

Situations reveal our praxis if we know how to read them. Praxis, as opposed to theory, is the actual situation with its deeds and misdeeds, its intentions and lack of intentions. Theory is a statement of how life and its situations might be or ought to be. Praxis is a form of reality testing in which our theories are scrutinized. We are not given a passing grade for good intentions. Rather we are tested for the honesty of our commitments and how they actually affect our lives.

This chapter attempts to pin down the praxis and theory of pastoral care in these post–Vatican II days. Behind much current pastoral praxis and theory there may be unsuspected and inadequate theologies of conversion, commitment to the work of the gospel, and ministry. To understand the persistence of such theologies some precedents in pastoral care in the pre–Vatican II period must be mentioned.

Case studies are one way of focusing on the praxis situations of pastoral care and its theologies. In order to concretize some of the theological concerns of this chapter let me propose one such case.

## The Case of Holy Cross Hospital

Holy Cross is a busy Catholic hospital in a large city. Under the progressive leadership of its administrators the pastoral care of the hospital has gradually evolved from the classical model of a priest-chaplain to a team model in which priests, sisters, and lay people share in the caring ministry. All the team members have received specialized theological and professional training and have been certified by the National Association of Hospital Chaplains.

Although the team works well together, tensions arise because of certain ministerial limitations imposed on the nonclerical members. After her frequent, extended, and helpful counseling sessions with a dying person, for example, Sister Margaret is not permitted to celebrate the sacraments of reconciliation and anointing of the sick with the patient. Instead she must invite Father Carroll to provide the sacramental dimension of ministry even though her own acquaintance with and care for the patient would perhaps have made her the more appropriate person to administer the sacraments. Does this case involve simply the question of the ordination of women, or are there other theological implications in this praxis situation?

The case of Holy Cross Hospital, manifesting as it does an obvious tension between ordained and nonordained ministry, suggests some far-reaching theological implications. In the first place both the patients and the members of the community operate with certain assumed definitions of salvation that spell out what they expect pastoral care to accomplish. For Roman Catholics in particular, priestly sacramental ministry has long been the major component in any definition of pastoral care.[1] In other words, sacraments form an important part of salvation, and therefore, of pastoral care. But normally in the Roman Catholic church the administrator of most sacraments is a bishop or a priest.

Also implied are the various understandings of church that Sister Margaret, Father Carroll, and the patient may have. For many people "church" is something they attend at times throughout the week, or "church" is the guardian of doctrine and dispenser of sacraments. They do not recognize their own place and mission as a constitutive element in the definition of church or salvation.

These implicit attitudes also shape the operative definitions of pastoral care. The patient, for example, may expect pastoral care to include comfort and reassurance but not a new sense of commitment to the work of the gospel. The priest may be operating with this same basic understanding even though it is articulated in a more sophisticated way in terms of a theology of grace and sacrament.

The distinction between our theoretical definitions and our operative definitions of salvation, church, and pastoral care is important if we are to analyze correctly the pastoral care scene since Vatican II. On first glance, we might be tempted to think of Holy Cross Hospital as illustrative of the transition that has taken place in Catholic pastoral care over the last fifteen years. Holy Cross, for example, now defines and exercises pastoral care in terms of a team ministry. Its members are presumably trained in basic counseling skills, and no doubt participate in specialized workshops dealing with such issues as death and dying, and the psychological dimensions of a mastectomy. In brief, Holy Cross seems to present a contemporary model of pastoral care that exemplifies the theology of Vatican II. But this initial perception may be deceptive.

## Pastoral Care in
## Ecumenical Perspective

If we compare the Holy Cross model of pastoral care with that of other Christian churches today, we seem to discover an ecumenical consensus. Although some Christian churches may give less emphasis than the Roman Catholic community to the sacramental component of pastoral care, the interdisciplinary approach to care and the professional models of care are usually the same.

The common areas of concern are embraced under the general rubric of "practical theology" which Don Browning has defined as "the reflective process which the church pursues in its efforts to articulate the theological grounds of practical living in various areas such as work, sexuality, marriage, youth, aging, and death."[2] Pastoral theology is generally viewed as that branch of practical theology which deals with the ministries that enflesh the care and leadership of the community for the sake of both the individual and the mission of the church.[3]

In America a whole generation of Roman Catholic priests has become familiar with key images and phrases used by Protestant theologians of pastoral care. Seward Hiltner's image of "shepherding" to describe all the activities of pastoral ministry is well known.[4] William Clebsch and Charles Jaekle suggest that the tasks of pastoral care can be described in terms of healing, guiding, sustaining, and reconciling.[5] Roman Catholic students of Hiltner, such as Henri Nouwen, have developed these perspectives within their own tradition.[6]

This ecumenical consensus in pastoral care stands in marked contrast to the pre–Vatican II period when the traditional Latin term for pastoral praxis and theory, *cura animarum* ("the cure or care of souls"), certainly had variant meanings for the various Christian traditions. A reading of John T. McNeill's classic, *A History of the Cure of Souls*, will quickly remind the reader that these different meanings were the result of more than simply divergent emphases, for example, on either the sacraments or preaching.[7] At times, there seem also to have been different definitions of salvation.

By contrast, the post–Vatican II period has seen a growing rapprochement between Roman Catholic and Protestant pastoral care. The emerging pastoral consensus began with a Roman Catholic appreciation of certain Protestant theologians (such as Daniel Day Williams, Hiltner, and Paul Pruyser) and adoption of certain Protestant-inspired training models (such as that of the Clinical Pastoral Education movement). This consensus has gradually broadened as theological dialogue between the churches began to yield results after long years of patient work.

## Temptations Connected with the Professional Model

After surveying some of the ecumenical consensus in pastoral praxis and theory, it may sound ungrateful to describe the post–Vatican II gains as "deceptive" from the viewpoint of Roman Catholic pastoral theology. The term is intended not to detract from the real advances made in pastoral theology since the Second Vatican Council but only to refer to the impasses in certain areas of current praxis and theory in Roman Catholic pastoral theology.

One such area involves the use of professional models of ministry, which have had a strong influence in all the Christian churches. A recent study entitled *Ministry in America* surveyed forty-seven denominations to learn what functions of ministry are considered most important by the approximately five thousand respondents. Eleven basic themes—such as "open, affirming style," "caring for persons under stress," "theologian in life and thought," and "ministry from a personal commitment of faith"—emerged from the survey. These themes clearly represent a mixture of purely professional qualities—such as one might expect in a good therapist—and certain theological components.[8]

Professional training and accountability are obviously an important part of pastoral care today. But pastoral care, from a theological viewpoint, must be more than therapy. Does pastoral care that is based on a professional model, for instance, actually facilitate Christian conversion? To what extent does it evoke deeper commitment to the gospel mission? How does it concretely help us to welcome God's future here and now?

The first temptation in current understandings of pastoral care in terms of the professional model is to confuse psychological congruence with ongoing religious conversion. What is in question in both cases is personal experience, whether the experience of the individual or the experience of the community. But we are compelled to focus attention on the meaning and implications of our experience more by the demands of the gospel than by any psychological model deriving from Sigmund Freud or Carl Rogers. Pastoral care must deal with God's goals as they challenge our own. It must attend to conversion.

A second temptation in the modern definition of pastoral care is to describe in static terms the commitments that conversion involves at each stage of our lives. Conversion, after all, entails more than the acceptance of creeds and the reception of sacraments. Conversion is the continuing experience of that to which Paul was referring when he said, "How deep are the riches and the wisdom and the knowledge of God! How inscrutable his judgments, how unsearchable his ways!" (Rom. 11:33).[9] Any adequate definition of pastoral care must allow for the dynamic character of such conversion. It must attend to commitment.

A third temptation in defining pastoral care, especially when employing professional models of ministry, is to mute transcendence. As Karl Rahner has noted, transcendence demands "the subjective, unthematic, necessary, and unfailing consciousness of the known subject that is co-present in every spiritual act of knowledge, and the subject's openness to the unlimited expanse of all possible reality."[10] But besides limiting God to the parameters of human definition, we may forget that God's presence—the source of all pastoral care—is discovered precisely in our human experience. Pastoral care in its fullest sense must attend to transcendence.

We will be discussing these three temptations throughout the book. My purpose in summarizing them here is to underscore the ultimate temptation of pastoral care—to substitute the clear and necessary professional model of human care for unarticulated definitions of salvation and the types of caring discipleship they must evoke. In this post–Vatican II period we must clearly distinguish between the professional gains we have made in trying to accomplish the work of the gospel, and the kind of theology our pastoral praxis actually implies.

## VATICAN II AND PASTORAL CARE

Although Vatican II did not give us a developed theology of pastoral care, it did juxtapose familiar and new theological understandings of church and mission and thereby suggested new directions for thinking about pastoral care. A first reading of the conciliar documents might give the impression that pastoral care is still identified almost exclusively with the ordained ministries of bishop and priest. A closer reading, however, reveals the larger contexts of pastoral activity within the church.

### Enlarged Contexts

The first of these larger contexts is evangelization.[11] Church and ministry exist not for their own sake but for the sake of Christ's work. The council presents a cosmic view of this work:

> Christ's redemptive work, while of itself directed toward the salvation of men, involves also the renewal of the whole temporal order. Hence the mission of the Church is not only to bring men to the message and grace of Christ, but also to penetrate and perfect the temporal sphere with the spirit of the Gospel. In fulfilling this mission of the Church, the laity therefore exercise their apostolate both in the Church and in the world, in both the spiritual and temporal orders.[12]

An enlarged concept of evangelization and mission is pivotal for any attempt to return to a more biblical definition of pastoral care. Without this larger context other conciliar statements—for example, "The parish exists solely for the good of souls"[13]—are misinterpreted and result in a theologically narrow conception of pastoral care.

A second conciliar context for understanding pastoral care is the so-called general priesthood of the faithful. Vatican II prefaces its discussion of the ordained ministry of the priesthood with a restatement of this teaching from 1 Peter:

> The Lord Jesus . . . has made his whole Mystical Body share in the anointing by the Spirit with which he himself has been anointed. For in him all the faithful are made a holy and royal priesthood. They offer spiritual sacrifices to God through Jesus Christ, and they proclaim the perfections of him who has called them out of darkness into his marvelous light. *Hence, there is no member who does not have a part in the mission of the whole Body.* Rather, each one ought to hallow Jesus in his heart and bear witness to Jesus in the Spirit of prophecy.[14]

In the "Dogmatic Constitution on the Church" (*Lumen Gentium*) the council, after making similar statements about the priesthood of all the baptized and the consequent call to witness to Christ, reiterates the distinction between this general priesthood of the faithful and the ministerial priesthood: "They differ from one another in essence and not only in degree. . . . Each of them in its own special way is a participation in the one priesthood of Christ."[15]

Joseph Komonchak has cogently argued in his analysis of Vatican II's teaching on mission and ministries that "the obscurities and difficulties in the council's view of the church-world and clergy-laity distinctions derive . . . from an incomplete reflection on the church's new situation in a secularized world and from a consequently ineffective pastoral response."[16] In emphasizing the general priesthood of all the faithful, I certainly do not intend—any more than did the council itself—to denigrate the specific tasks of mission traditionally assigned to the ordained ministries of bishop and priest, but when this general priesthood has historically been lost sight of, the result has always been an impoverishment of the central idea of mission and its implementation in both ordained and nonordained ministries.[17] As David Power has pointed out, even this statement of the general mission of all the initiated does not dispel the conciliar ambiguity concerning the roles of laity and clergy.[18] The laity's role is still seen as operative in the secular sphere.[19] It is true that this role is somewhat expanded in paragraph 33 of the "Dogmatic Constitution on the Church" where more directed cooperation with the "apostolate of the hierarchy" is envisaged.[20] There is a theological ambiguity here that can probably be traced to the presence of more than one ecclesiology in the teaching of Vatican II.[21]

## Deepened Meaning

What emerges from these larger questions of mission and general priesthood is a reconsideration of the meaning of pastoral care for both the ordained and nonordained ministries. Pastoral care must, in biblical language, enable the blind to see and the deaf to hear, so that they in turn may similarly enable others. We pastorally care for one another so that we may proclaim what the Lord is doing among us. As the blind man, healed by Christ, begins to follow him "giving God the glory" (Luke 18:43), so there is no one healed for his or her own sake; all are healed for the sake of Christ's ongoing mission.

In initiation each Christian is individually called to service and mission. That is the point of Paul's teaching about the continuing call to be Christian: as Christ, so we (Rom. 6:4). As Christ was sent to heal and to proclaim the good news (Mark 1:38), so each Christian is sent.

Ecclesiologies that in praxis value the institutional or private dimensions of church over the tasks of mission often lead to a loss of focus. The church and its ministries can become an end in themselves. The Christ who is in our midst "as the one who serves" (Luke 22:27) can be forgotten.

There is a tension in the theology of Vatican II between a jurisdictional ecclesiology and a patristic communion ecclesiology, and this tension is not a purely academic issue.[22] It betrays itself in the everyday praxis of pastoral care in a parish, a hospital, or a campus ministry. The priorities of time and effort actually set in such ministries disclose the implicit understandings of salvation, church, and mission held by the communities and ministers who exercise them. Simply to allow the laity wider jurisdiction in ministry does not of itself address these deeper issues.

The case of Holy Cross Hospital can again serve as a concrete example. Sister Margaret is classified among the laity as far as the sacramental ministry is concerned. In effect, her situation illustrates the dichotomized ecclesiology of Vatican II. However, even if Sister Margaret were to receive ordination and canonical faculties to minister the sacraments of reconciliation and anointing, this would not solve the underlying issues of the situation: What must pastoral care evoke—from both the minister and the persons ministered unto—in the way of evangelization and renewed commitment to mission?[23] Does the parish community to which this hospital patient belongs have a real use for the charisms of its members? Is the team ministry at the hospital an example, in praxis, of a jurisdictional ecclesiology, that is, a group of ministers who *function* together but who do not commune with and enable one another? (This last question is more than just a theological version of the question as to whether the team is actually operating with a positive group dynamics.)

What is traditionally said of the priest's pastoral care can, without any confusion of ordained and nonordained ministries, be properly said of all the baptized:

"Pastoral care" describes the priest's relationship of service to people in need. . . . The full person of the priest is brought to the tasks of pastoral care, but it is the Lord who cares for us all who is proclaimed. . . . Pastoral care ranges in expression, limited only by the wants of the people. . . . And yet, it cannot be expected that each priest is qualified for every task or that each priest is capable of responding to the myriad of pastoral needs.[24]

The question that emerges from such a description is this: How are these gifts of service evoked from the Christian community and what praxis model can help us constantly to clarify the purpose of pastoral care in our midst? The early Christian church may offer a pastoral answer in that process of becoming Christian which has long been known as the catechumenate.

## THE CATECHUMENATE AS A MODEL OF PASTORAL CARE

As early as the middle of the second century, when baptism and confirmation were still one initiation sacrament, many communities were already employing a challenging process of formation for candidates wishing to become Christian—the catechumenate. The origins of the process lay as much in the enormous pastoral task of forming Christian attitudes and life styles in a hostile environment as it did in assuring orthodox teaching of the faith. In effect, a local church had to attend to two continuing pastoral concerns—the credibility of the Christian community's commitment, and an effective gospel challenge to interested pagans and Jews.

It is obvious from the letters of Paul that initiation alone did not assure the continuing fidelity of new Christians. The gospel values of love and service were only partially appropriated by some converts. This situation in turn presented a pastoral dilemma for those in charge of preparing candidates for initiation into the Christian community: the gospel ideals being taught to candidates for initiation were not always being fully lived out by those already baptized. If the catechumenate was to be effective, it would have to address the renewal of the baptized as much as the preparation of new candidates.[25]

### Ongoing Process

· A major concern of pastoral care was thus the catechumenal effort to renew the commitment of the baptized while evoking commitment from the nonbaptized candidates. To accomplish this goal a process of interaction between the baptized and the catechumens was set in motion.[26] Christians and candidates together were involved in a process of continuing education in which key aspects of the gospel message came to be appreciated from a new vantage point.

We have already mentioned the Pauline summary of what Christian initiation entails: as Christ, so we (Rom. 6:4). Paul is describing an identification process in which someone becomes Christian *in praxis.* The catechumenate spelled out this teaching in concrete terms for a specific group of Christians living in a particular context.

In the third-century *Apostolic Tradition* of Hippolytus, for example, the community evokes initial commitment from interested pagans by demanding that they give up certain types of work that might contradict the values of the gospel (for example, prostitution, or civil or military responsibilities that could entail the perpetration of injustice). Candidates who are elected into the long catechumenal process (normally three years in the *Apostolic Tradition*) have two major sources for learning the Christian way—the proclaimed Word of God and the experience of a tightly knit Christian community.

Both the Word of God and the way it was actually being lived out now in the community called into question the way the catechumens had formerly understood their needs and goals. Catechumens began to learn new ways to pray and to minister to the needs of others, ways that reflected their new experiences of the presence of God in their lives. The frequent laying on of hands and repeated exorcisms were a complement to this gradual process of discovering their redemptive needs and the ways in which God had gifted them to build up the body of Christ. Changes in life goals and styles, in choice of friends and jobs were the practical corollaries of conversion. The catechumenate called forth and supported these new ways. Long after initiation into the Christian community, the process of integration into its life and work continued. To put it in modern terms, praxis theology was an important formational element in becoming Christian.

No Christian community could remain unaffected by such a process going on in its midst. The commitment of the catechumens challenged that of the baptized. The catechumens' new sense of mission and service called in question that of the rest of the Christian community. In other words, not only the catechumen but the whole community was once again invited into the rites of passage which are the heart of any communal renewal.[27]

### Theological Implications

Even evident from this cursory description of the catechumenate are the implications of such a process for a theology of pastoral care. Effective pastoral care is the catechumenal model in dynamic action. For ultimately pastoral care, as all efforts of the Christian community, must help us appropriate and implement our baptismal commitment. Ultimately, therefore, pastoral care helps us to concretize our operative definitions of salvation, church, sin, mission, and ministry.

*Salvation*

"Salvation" as defined in the catechumenal process is experienced both as the unearned presence of God and as our continuing response to that presence. Pastoral care is the practical expression of that teaching. It helps us identify the forms of commitment to the gospel-life that are needed in our particular social and personal situation. In the case of Holy Cross Hospital, for example, the pastoral care that Sister Margaret gives to dying patients need not call in question either her or their theoretical definitions of salvation.

But such care must help the Christian patient to respond to God's presence with new meaning at a final turning point in life. Such care must assist the dying Christian to realize anew that while God's love remains unearned, it enables us "to rouse each other to love and good deeds" (Heb. 10:24).

*Church*

A Christian community with church catechumens in its midst saw ecclesiology in praxis, and therefore understood how church was to be defined. Central to Paul's teaching is the belief that all the baptized are called to build up the body of Christ (1 Cor. 12). In turn the Christian community as the body of Christ does not exist for its own sake. It has the privileged mission of proclaiming the gospel. Catechumens learned such key doctrines by seeing them lived out in the priorities of the community, where all were expected to care for the sick, visit the imprisoned, open up their homes to traveling Christians, and spread the good news.

By contrast, not all pastoral care has encouraged similar ecclesial awareness. Although recipients of such care, such as the elderly, the sick, the oppressed or underprivileged, might appreciate the local church's outreach to them, do these pastoral ministries elicit service from the served? Do such people relearn the Pauline teaching about their responsibility for building up the ecclesial community, or are they rather only confirmed in their tendency to remain passive members of the church? The catechumenal model suggests a rethinking of the ways in which pastoral care can and should teach people in praxis what ecclesiology actually means for them at a particular stage of their lives.

*Sin*

Once Christians learn to appreciate the ways in which God has gifted them for the sake of others, however, it immediately becomes easier to detect the traces of radical and personal sin in their own experience. In the catechumenal process sin is not a theological abstraction but rather the perceived alternative to a life lived out in Christian commitment.

Again, pastoral care has much to learn from such a process. Effective pastoral care helps Christians to define in concrete terms the radical sin of their sociocultural situation. Expressions of radical sin, for example, can differ markedly, as in the prejudices so easily tolerated among white and nonwhite Christians in a certain part of town, or in the respectable materialism of another part of the same town. Personal sin is revealed in all its deforming tendencies only when seen against the background of the contexts, crises, and challenges of each life stage of the individual. Historically, pastoral care has always been most authentic when, in place of abstract definitions or lists of sin, it has provided a process whereby Christians can begin to see both their own sin and God's power actually enfleshed in the concrete experience of their own world.

*Mission and Ministry*

Finally, from the moment they began to walk the Christian way catechumens learned the meaning of being sent ("mission") and of service ("ministry"). One striking example of this is seen in the spread of Christianity among the Roman armies. Roman martyrology is replete with the names of individual soldiers as well as whole cohorts who bore witness to their faith even unto death. The only plausible explanation for this rapid evangelization among these fighting men is the ministry of their fellow Christian soldiers.[28] Many were still catechumens at the time they were martyred.

A pastoral care that does not renew in people an appropriate sense of mission and ministry is questionable. It fosters in praxis dubious, self-centered notions of salvation. True care from a gospel viewpoint invites both young and old to share in the work of building the kingdom of God. The dying Christian, for example, has an important ministry to fulfill. Death, for many, arouses fear because this inevitable event of human living threatens to destroy all meaning. Christians who can die with meaning witness more to the good news than any sermon or theological book on the subject of death and dying. But does our pastoral care call forth such ministry from the dying Christian?

## SOME CONCLUSIONS

"Professional" in current American usage is an ambiguous term. In today's work world the word implies at least some specialized learning for specific tasks and some peer control and accountability.[29] The term also includes the interpersonal relationship between the professional and the client.[30] Pastoral care in a more restricted sense is the work of professionals, that is, people who have received the training to accomplish certain specialized tasks in Christian ministry.

Theology, however, cannot start from this more restricted understanding of pastoral care.[31] Any ministry of the Christian community reveals in its praxis the implicit definitions—historically and psychosocially conditioned definitions—of salvation and church. Edward Schillebeeckx has recently demonstrated how each Christian epoch, with varying degrees of success, has dealt with these dimensions in its definitions of ministry.[32]

The theologian notes with interest that "professional" and "profess" have the same Latin root: *fateri* means "to confess, or reveal." In a theological sense pastoral care is concerned with the Christian profession, that is, both the revelation of and the response to God's unearned love and its power. The purpose of pastoral care is to heal and support us as we walk together toward the kingdom of God so that we might do the work of the gospel. In brief, pastoral care must confront the praxis of our lives.

This conviction has shaped the argument of this chapter: praxis contains the operative definitions of salvation, church, sin, and mission which pastoral care must confront and question. Historically the theory of pastoral care has too often assumed these definitions, and thus bypassed the redemptive problems to deal only with the symptoms. In the case of Holy Cross Hospital the pressing pastoral question is not, Who is the appropriate minister of a sacrament? but What are the pastoral needs of both the team ministry and of the several patients, each with their own unique experiences?

As a first attempt to reexamine such praxis issues from a theological viewpoint, I have proposed the catechumenal model. The catechumenate, recently restored within the Roman Catholic community as the normal process of adult initiation,[33] is a model of pastoral care because (1) it challenges the praxis and theory of both the baptized and the candidates, (2) it uncovers the operative definitions implicit in our praxis so that the pastoral care actually required might be better focused, and (3) it defines all pastoral care within the larger theological context of our baptismal commitment. As we shall see in the next chapter, there is a marked contrast between the theology of pastoral care implicit in the catechumenal process and some pre–Vatican II theologies of pastoral care.

The Protestant reader, bringing a somewhat different theology and praxis to the reading of this opening chapter, will nonetheless discover some worthwhile questions emerging from this discussion of Roman Catholic developments. The first such question derives from the increasingly shared model of professional training. Does it help us to discern the common theological concerns that undergird our similar pastoral care activities? To what extent do we experience the same theological temptations in our ecumenical forms of professional pastoral care?

A more specific ecumenical question has to do with whether our pastoral care praxis is helping us arrive at a new consensus with respect to such theological issues as mission, the role of the laity, and the church. Biblical scholarship has certainly helped to forge a widening agreement on these issues, but has our pastoral care praxis supported this tendency? For example, does the emphasis in Roman Catholic pastoral care on building an ecclesial community that is in mission "for the sake of others" dispel some of the theological fears of sixteenth-century Protestants about the role of a visible church in God's justifying action in this world? The ecumenical thrust of these questions may be sharpened as they are developed in subsequent chapters.

## CHAPTER 2

# Pre–Vatican II Theologies
# of
# Pastoral Care

In moments of discouragement anyone involved in pastoral care would do well to read the laments of Salvian, a fifth-century priest:

> We hold and cast aside the faith, and we confess the gift of salvation equally as we deny it. Where, therefore, is our Christianity, we who receive the sacrament of salvation only for the purpose that we may sin afterwards with the greater crime of deviation from righteousness? We prefer stage plays to the churches of God. We spurn altars and honor the theaters. We love things and worship things. God alone, in comparison with all other things, is vile to us.[1]

Pastoral care, in every century, has had to deal with the imperfect commitment of the Christian community and its members. In Salvian's fifth-century Gaul the catechumenate and canonical penance were already in decline. Since the early fourth century large numbers of converts had swelled the membership of the average Christian community. As we can easily gather from the sermons of pastors such as Augustine or Caesar of Arles, there were in such communities many noncommitted and passive Christians.

Alongside the professional, ordained groups of ministries that developed in the church, the informal, nonordained ministries of pastoral care—teaching, visiting the sick, and counseling—also continued. But as the catechumenate and canonical penance diminished in their capacity effectively to call forth quality of commitment in initiation and of recommitment in penance, there was a tendency to rely on the ordained ministries to do the work of the gospel. In other words pastoral care came to be seen as something done by the clergy or religious. The pastoral scene was further complicated by the developing notion of jurisdiction—the juridical equivalent of discerning charisms and ministries in the community. These subtle but significant changes had important implications for pastoral care.

This chapter is neither a history of pastoral care nor a review of the theologies of pastoral care. Rather, it attempts to trace the praxis of pastoral care as seen in the sacrament of reconciliation and penance. This sacrament is crucial in renewing the baptismal commitment of Christians in any age. If this commitment is not renewed then the conception and praxis of pastoral care becomes the work of professionals rather than the shared undertaking of the whole Christian community.

Gabriel Le Bras noted some years ago that a history of the praxis of pastoral care in each period of the church's life had yet to be written.[2] Not surprisingly, the theories of pastoral care in any particular age do not always correspond with the praxis of the same period. In Paul's theory of pastoral care, for example, all Christians are to use their gifts to build up the body of Christ; the community has the responsibility to discern these gifts and their use. Yet the praxis situation of pastoral care in Paul's communities required that he give consideration and space to it in some of his letters.

Disparities between theory and praxis are to be found also in succeeding centuries. Attempts to clarify the role of ordained ministries and their exercise (jurisdiction) often led unwittingly in praxis to a narrowing of the notion of pastoral care—indeed frequently to lessened commitment and a limited pastoral care. In our age, with its diminishing numbers of clergy and its increasing need for effective pastoral care, we can perhaps learn something from a brief review of the historical developments.

## CHARISM AND OFFICE

Pastoral care has always relied on two resources—charisms and ministries. Charisms are usually associated with the unique gifts given to each individual for building up the Christian community. Ministries are the result of discerned needs and roles in the mission of the community; often they become ordained offices in the church. There has always been a temptation to describe the development of ministries in the early church in terms of office gradually replacing charism. To a certain extent this is in fact what happened, but such a simple description does not adequately portray the richness and complexity of the actual development.[3]

In 1 Corinthians and Romans we discover a pastoral dynamic,

based on mutual love, in which charisms have a function that is complementary to other services and ministries for building up the body of Christ. In a typical passage Paul says:

> Just as each of us has one body with many members, and not all the members have the same function, so too we, though many, are one body in Christ and individually members of one another. We have gifts that differ according to the favor bestowed on each of us. One's gift may be prophecy; its use should be in proportion to his faith. It may be the gift of ministry; it should be used for service. One who is a teacher should use his gift for teaching; one with the power of exhortation should exhort. He who gives alms should do so generously; he who rules should exercise his authority with care; he who performs works of mercy should do so cheerfully. Your love must be sincere. . . . Do not grow slack but be fervent in spirit; he whom you serve is the Lord. (Rom. 12:4–11)

In these verses, as Ernst Käsemann points out, charism and office are not yet separated. As long as each gift is tempered by a sense of service, the community is not afraid to recognize the authority of each charism.[4]

By the time the pastoral letters were written, however, in the last quarter of the first century, the growing complexity of some of the larger Christian communities demanded more institutionalized ministries.[5] The description of some offices in 1 Timothy 3, for example, has a familiar ring. Timothy is present as a leader who is charismatic: "Do not neglect the gift you received when, as a result of prophecy, the presbyters laid their hands on you" (1 Tim. 4:14). The presidency of the Eucharist seems to be a normal part of the leader's role in the community.[6] But what we know of these communities seems to indicate that each Christian was expected to take part in the mission of the gospel in a way appropriate to his or her gifts and situation.

Despite the inevitable problems attendant upon the growing institutionalization of the Christian community, pastoral care probably flourished in the first three centuries because of the quality of commitment demanded by intermittent persecution and social isolation. The Roman Christian community with its various heretics and Cyprian's Carthaginian community with its internal ministerial struggles could still boast of its martyrs, the mutual care of its members, and an evangelization shared in by the whole community.

With the Constantinian toleration of and then favoritism toward Christianity in the fourth century, new dangers emerged. The catechumenates began to be filled with candidates whose social or political motivation was an obstacle to their accepting the mission of the gospel. Bishops were increasingly expected to fulfill some of the administrative responsibilities of the empire. The size of individual Christian communities swelled considerably. The dynamics that evoked shared pastoral care at Corinth in A.D. 54 or at Ephesus in A.D. 75 could not be so easily maintained at Rome or Carthage in A.D. 400.

What is important to remember for the history of pastoral care is that charisms and ministries continued to strengthen average Christian communities, not only during the times of isolation and persecution but also during the new era of toleration and favor. We gradually begin to hear more about offices in the church, however, possibly because for organizational purposes the increasingly large ecclesial communities tended to rely more on the institutionalized charisms of the bishop than the individual charisms of the prophet or confessor. But it is interesting that Martin of Tours in the fourth century still combined many of the traditional dimensions of charism and office, of prophet and bishop, of pastoral leadership and care.

## POWER AND PASTORAL CARE

By the fifth century the average bishop found himself in much the same situation as Augustine, with a good part of his day spent in administrative detail, in arbitrating disputes, and in maintaining a civil as well as an ecclesial presence in the community.[7] Bernard Cooke has pointed out, however, that throughout this period, when the roles of bishop and priests were expanding, the basic ministries of hospitality, healing, and care of the poor remained a major concern and responsibility.[8] Pastoral care inspired the foundation of a number of religious communities. Committed lay Christians continued to perform the spiritual and corporal works of mercy which we regard today as concrete manifestations of pastoral care.

But in both theory and praxis the work of the ordained ministries in pastoral care was increasingly associated with the sacramental dimension of church life and its canonical regulation. Up to this time the image of shepherd-leader had been shaped by such models of Christian commitment and care as Ignatius of Antioch in the second century, Cyprian in the third century, and Martin of Tours in the fourth century.[9] In the case of each of these bishops the sacramental dimension of their ministries was indeed prominent. But as church office became more juridically conceived, the definition of pastoral care became more limited.

Gregory the Great, for example, in his classic *Pastoral Care* (c. 590) describes the pastoral office as *"the government of souls . . . the art of arts."*[10] While his book reveals in many ways a biblical sense of ministry, the principal metaphor throughout is that of the ruler. As in the tenth-century rituals, there is a sense of ordained ministry as service coupled with more juridical images that mirror the real working world of many feudal bishops. In the same way, as we move from the third-century *Apostolic Tradition* of Hippolytus with its ritual of episcopal consecration to that of the Romano-Germanic pontifical of the tenth century, the cultic, the pastoral, and the juridical developments in the theology of ministry are accurately reflected.[11]

Another factor destined to affect pastoral care directly is the developing canonical distinction between the power of orders and the power of jurisdiction. The power of orders is conceived as the ability to do specific ministerial tasks (for example, the power to bind and loose, to celebrate the Eucharist), while the power of jurisdiction indicates when and where these abilities may be exercised (for example, when and where and by whom the sacrament of penance may be celebrated). The bishop has both powers and, in turn, signifies the power given to a priest in ordination by the symbolic handing over of the paten and chalice and of the vestments. The bishop will presumably allow the use of these powers conferred (jurisdiction) within certain bounds. (We will discuss these powers in relation to penance as pastoral care in the next section.)

Medieval discussions of the care of souls centered around the question of whether such care is linked with the power of orders or with the power of jurisdiction. The operative canonical word is *executio*, the use of the power given. In one sense, jurisdiction is the medieval attempt to discern charisms within the highly institutionalized structures of the church.

The canonical solution seems strange to our post–Vatican II ears but it is a logical conclusion to the canonical concept of pastoral care. The power to give absolution in the sacrament of penance, for example, is viewed as central to the care of souls. This requires the power of orders. A nonpriest could also have the care of souls and thus be able, for example, to excommunicate and dispense. Yet even in this case a priest was required for confession. G. Fransen sums up these canonical developments by citing the influential juridical definition of pastoral care by Antoninus (1459): Pastoral care is *"a certain power over subjects,* in conferring sacraments on them oneself or through another and in doing those things which pertain to the salvation of souls such as correction and the like."[12]

To view these developments as simply another example of institutionalization would be to miss the central point—namely, the historical effort to effect a balance between the biblical notion of charisms as God-given abilities to serve the mission of the ecclesial community (power) and the need to discern these charisms and their use (jurisdiction). David Power has rephrased the question in terms of power and authority:

> The more juridically the office is conceived, the more easily *power* and *authority* are confused into one notion. The more charismatically it is conceived, the more readily the place of ordination can be seen as an action of the church or the particular community which is a sacramental recognition of a *power* already possessed with the conferring of the kind of *authority* that this brings with it, so that the office-holder can better serve the community and its mission through the use of his *powers* in the appropriate social and sacramental context.[13]

In every century since the time of Christ the Christian church has tried to follow the Pauline admonition to discern and use all gifts to build up the body of Christ (1 Cor. 12 and 14). Even when the juridical perspective of ministry and pastoral care predominated over the more-biblical dimensions of service and mission which stem from the general priesthood of the faithful, there has always been an awareness of and concern for pastoral care on every level of the church's life. But history has more than that to teach us.

A juridical view of office which forgets power (*exousia*) in the biblical sense—as the unearned gift to serve, given by God alone, for the sake of others—is not able accurately to discern the use of this power. The pastoral result is that the community fails to call forth new service from its members or feels compelled to restrict service in pastoral care. On the other hand, the actual praxis of pastoral care historically has sometimes been able to challenge theories and theologies of pastoral care. The discussion of penance as pastoral care is one historical example.

## PENANCE AS PASTORAL CARE

In one sense John T. McNeill is correct in treating pastoral care during the first six Christian centuries exclusively under the rubric of penance.[14] The penance of those early centuries involved large pastoral issues such as commitment and the understandings of salvation and of the mission of the church. In nearly two thousand years of pastoral care the Christian community has struggled to deal with just such questions of motivation and commitment, conversion and witness in the lives of all its members. The purpose of this section is not to repeat the extensive history of the sacrament given by McNeill and others but to draw out its implications for a contemporary theology of pastoral care.

In chapter 1 I proposed the catechumenate as the basic Christian model of ongoing initiation into the responsibilities of being Christian. But as Salvian would testify many of the catechumens, once initiated, did not continue to deepen their commitment to the gospel. As naive as it might seem to us, earlier Christian communities did not anticipate this difficulty. Nevertheless their pastoral care had to be redefined in light of it.

In the Letter to the Hebrews and in other early Christian writers, such as the second-century Hermas, we find the same reaction to the presence of sinful and even uncommitted Christians in the community. This reaction is understandable only if we keep in mind the expectation of these early Christians about the imminent return of Christ and the mutuality forged by small and isolated groups of committed people. Here then is one of the earliest tests of pastoral care in the young Christian communities: Is it possible for those who have fallen away from a faithful gospel-life to repent again?

As we move into the third century the pastoral question changes due to the human weakness of many Christians under intense persecution: How can faltering Christians be invited to conversion and commitment a second time? Both laxist and rigorist attitudes within the Christian communities make this question pastorally difficult to work out in praxis. After official toleration and then favor is accorded the Christian church in the fourth century, the pastoral problem emerges once more in a new form: How can large groups of Christians, with widely different motivations, be encouraged to do penance?

If we look at the way in which the church dealt with the problem of serious sinners in the first six centuries, there seems to be an interesting similarity between the catechumenal and the penitential process. First, because of the importance placed on Christian commitment there is what we might call a catechumenal hesitancy to accord an easy forgiveness for those types of serious sin that affected the whole community.

Tertullian, a third-century North African theologian who seems to have been actively involved in the catechumenate at Carthage, urges catechumens to persevere in the way of conversion: "What folly it is, what perversity, to practice an imperfect penitence and then to expect a pardon for sin! *This is to stretch forth one's hand for merchandise and not to pay the price.*"[15] He then turns to the case of sinful Christians and holds out one more chance, saying that God "has permitted the door of forgiveness, although it is closed and locked by the bar of baptism, still to stand somewhat open. He has placed in the vestibule a second penitence so that it may open the door to those who knock; *only once, however, because it is already a second time.*"[16]

To appreciate this insistence on commitment, the reader today has to keep in mind that only certain sins (for example, adultery, apostasy, murder) required the formal penitential process that is called canonical penance. These sins were considered particularly destructive of the life and mission of the Christian community. For other sins, serious and less serious, Christians were expected to pray and fast, give alms to the poor, and engage in other works of mercy. In other words, serious public sin required canonical or public penance while hidden or private sins demanded private penance.[17]

But in the case of both repentant catechumens and sinful Christians, the underlying dynamic of pastoral care is the same—conversion that shows itself in renewed and grateful commitment. In contrast to Antoninus's late-medieval definition of pastoral care, cited in the preceding section, there is a strong emphasis in the catechumenal and penitential model to pay the price of commitment and thus imitate the servant of God, Christ.

## Penance in Transition

As the catechumenal process began to break down in the fourth century because of the influx of poorly motivated converts, so the penitential process began to break down because of a growing number of less-than-committed Christians. In fact, many families enrolled their male children as catechumens but delayed their initiation until adulthood so that they might have *two* chances to be reconciled—initiation and penance. Responding to a pastoral tendency to be more rigorous in preventing people from receiving this penance, the average Christian tended to delay formal penance until the moment of death.

Augustine complains that some fervent catechumens, shocked to see that in their daily lives baptized Christians were not as committed as themselves, postponed their own initiation.[18] By the sixth century Caesar of Arles is compelled constantly to warn the Christians of

Gaul against postponing penance. Because of the severity of canonical penance a deathbed conversion, to most people, seemed preferable. In response Caesar urges public penance upon those of whom penance is required, mentioning the benefit they can derive from the support of the Christian community: "As a matter of fact, one who does public penance could have performed it privately. However, after considering the multitude of his sins, he feels that he is not strong enough to oppose his great vices alone, and so he wants to solicit the assistance of all the people."[19]

If the majority of Christians postponed formal penance, what then should they do until their deathbed? Again Caesar of Arles reminds his listeners that if they have sinned seriously, they can show their repentance and receive forgiveness by their good works, tithes, and daily love of both enemies and friends. He concludes: "If a man is willing to fulfill this, he will die well because he has always fruitfully and devoutly done penance even though he does not formally receive it."[20]

Corresponding to this general penitential advice there emerged a form of pastoral care that had probably always been present in some form in the Christian community but gained new impetus under the influence of monasticism—spiritual direction. For the many Christians who postponed the severe penance that led to formal reconciliation with the church, there was the opportunity to discuss their current situation and how they might become better Christians.

Just as monks who could not enter canonical or public penance benefited from a discussion of their sins and weaknesses with their abbot, so laypeople were encouraged to seek similar help. Benedict advises his monks: "If, however, guilt of his offense be hidden in his own soul, let him manifest it to the abbot only, or to his spiritual seniors who know how to heal their wounds, and will not disclose or publish those of others."[21] The abbot would pray for the monk's forgiveness and assign a penance. These monastic practices, adopted by pious Christians in some parts of the West, represented a realistic pastoral care approach at a time when penance was in transition.

There is much that we can learn from canonical penance in our attempts to care pastorally for each other today. First, although the history of penance in the first six centuries is complex, one fact emerges quite clearly: Penance, as pastoral care, is the concern of the whole community. The bishop is ideally the leader and principal discerner of both the catechumenal and penitential process. But as the catechumenate demands the guidance of sponsors, the teaching of catechumenal teams, and the prayerful intervention of the whole community, so the penitential process implies a communal ministry.

The Christian community, seeing penitents at the door of the church or kneeling in their midst, were reminded to support these fellow Christians by prayer and action. In turn, average Christians were challenged by the example of both catechumens and penitents to reexamine their own commitments to gospel-faith and gospel-living. In a very real sense, the whole community was pastorally cared for as they attended to the needy ones in their midst.

A second instructive dimension of canonical penance derives from its therapeutic character. As we have seen, it was the nonclerical monastic practice of the leader or of an elder discerning the spiritual situation of the monk that served as a model during the transition period when canonical penance was declining. Just as laypeople had served as part of the catechumenal teams even in Tertullian's time, so nonclerical spiritual direction was used to great advantage without detracting from the ordained ministries within the community.

Third, by the time of the fifth and sixth centuries pastoral care had to deal with the results of three centuries of sometimes indiscriminate initiation, whereby Christian communities were filled with varying types of committed and noncommitted Christians—a scene not dissimilar to our own. The penitential process, with all its weaknesses, represented a pastoral effort to elicit continuing conversion and commitment from all its members. Whether Christians were among the minority enrolled officially among the penitents, or sought discernment and direction for their lives at the urging of the preaching and under the example of saintly leaders and fellow Christians, there was an ongoing renewal of the commitments of initiation.

## The Irish Tariff

Pastoral care, when effective, is usually well attuned to the social and historical situation in which it operates. The praxis of canonical penance in the sixth century indirectly underscores this principle. Pastoral praxis at that time was at an impasse in matters penitential. The severity of the old penitential system prompted Christians to postpone penance until they were on their deathbed. Bishops sought, paradoxically, to correct this reaction by making the penitential process even more restrictive. The spiritual direction of more-committed Christians seems to have filled the pastoral vacuum in some places. In brief, the pastoral scene had changed but rituals and theologies had not kept pace with those changes.

This state of affairs only highlights the unique form of pastoral care that was evolving in the sixth century in Ireland. The "Irish tax or tariff system," as it came to be called, was a process of renewed conversion and penance singularly suited to the social and historical situation of sixth-century Ireland. Even after the Christianization of Ireland, the wild Celtic character still proved a test of even the most-ascetic monastic system, as the lives of the early Irish saints testify. The only penitential system that would prove successful in this cultural milieu originates from what was then the predominant Christian force in Ireland—monasticism.

Soon after Patrick's time, the church of Ireland seems to have become a basically monastic church. Although bishops celebrated ordinations, it was the abbots who directed the ordinary life of both the monasteries and the larger Christian community. This was to prove crucial for the new pastoral praxis.

In a marvelous blending of pre-Christian Celtic law and monastic asceticism, Irish penance attempted to deal with Christian living on a day-to-day basis in much the same way that the chapter of faults and spiritual direction did for the monks. Penitents, like the monks, listed the sins and failings of their daily life. For each transgression a specific penance was given (hence the name "tax" or "tariff" penance). On the completion of the penance, the penitent returned to receive absolution. (In later times the penitent received immediate absolution on the promise of doing the penance.)

A whole literature, the so-called Irish penitentials, developed to help the confessor in assigning appropriate penances. It is in these penitentials that we see the creative use of pre-Christian Celtic customs such as the *anmchara* or "soul-friend," and the rules for satisfaction and substitution. Eastern monastic practices of correcting sinful life styles by encouraging the opposite behavior (the law of contraries) also found their way into the penitential system. Thus, the sixth-century penitential of Finnian rules: "But if a cleric is covetous, this is a great offense; covetousness is pronounced idolatry but it can be corrected by liberality and alms. This is the penance for his offense that he cure and correct contraries by contraries."[22]

Christians who today read the typical penance assigned for sins in this Irish system will be shocked by its apparent harshness. Sleeping in water or on nettles or with a dead body in a grave is recommended by the Old Irish Table of Commutations, for, as the document remarks, there are hardly any lay people who have "nor had a share in manslaughter."[23] For lesser faults, such as murmuring against "a good prince," one penitential calls for seven days on bread and water.[24]

Caution is needed in evaluating this approach. The severity of the Irish tax system, in its cultural setting, should not be confused with that of canonical penance. The Irish penance, unlike its European predecessor, could be repeated as often as needed. The Irish approach did not involve perpetual sexual abstinence and could be performed more privately than canonical penance. Above all, this penitential approach, rooted in Irish custom and realistic about the Celtic temperament, seems to have been pastorally successful for both monks and lay people.

In this process a creative use was made of the soul-friend, an institution that may have antedated Christianity. The Irish monk was expected to have a spiritual adviser with whom he could share everything. In earlier days this soul-friend was not necessarily a priest, though later penitentials usually required confession to a priest.

With theological and pastoral hindsight it is easy to indicate some of the negative aspects of the new penance. The penitentials, with their easily accumulated tariffs and the consequent need for commutation to lesser penances, promoted a certain juridical approach to conversion. The great emphasis on receiving absolution encouraged a short-range view of conversion in comparison with the long-term conversion demanded by canonical penance. More subtle and dangerous was a certain Pelagian tendency to earn one's salvation by the penance performed. Finally, the communal ecclesial nature of penance is more difficult to discern in Irish tax penance.

Although canonical and Irish tax penance both were, within their original cultural and historical contexts, successful in helping people appropriate their initiation commitment at later stages of their life, their pastoral effectiveness was diminished when these approaches to pastoral care later became formulas indiscriminately applied in other periods and cultures. This change of context usually resulted not only in diminished numbers of the faithful receiving the sacrament but more particularly in misplaced reasons behind the praxis of the sacrament.

It would be outside the purpose of this chapter to trace the transplanting of the Irish penance to the continent by Alcuin and other monastic missionaries after the barbarian devastations, and the subsequent development of the medieval "manuals of confessors."[25] By the thirteenth century it was obvious that penance as pastoral care had once again fallen into disuse; the Fourth Lateran Council (1215) felt constrained to legislate yearly confession for those in serious sin.

Medieval discussion of penance centered on the acts of the penitent (contrition, confession, satisfaction) and on absolution. John Duns Scotus, the great fourteenth-century Franciscan theologian, went so far as to define penance as "the *absolution* of a penitent, performed with certain words and due intention by a priest, possessing jurisdiction."[26]

What is sometimes missed in modern references to historical developments is the praxis situation. When canonical penance was directed by a bishop like Ambrose or Augustine—or the fervent Irish monks of the sixth and seventh centuries as confessors of the tax penance—penitential praxis was in good hands. But who can forget Chaucer's tale of the self-serving friar-confessor? In addition, medieval Europe had numbers of semi-literate mass priests who were not allowed to preach or hear confession.

By the sixteenth century the bishops and theologians at the Council of Trent in discussing the dearth of competent confessors bore eloquent testimony to the crisis in this dimension of pastoral care. Among the universally regarded abuses was the lack of training and selection for this ministry. The metaphor of the confessor as doctor (which we will discuss in the next chapter) was employed to examine the credibility of individuals who were sometimes in a worse spiritual condition than that of their penitents. The objection of some observers that even "bad spiritual doctors can absolve" only betrays some of the theological and pastoral deterioration in the area of penance.[27]

## PASTORAL CARE AS RENEWAL

Pastoral care can be treated, as McNeill and others have done, by outlining the historical development of penance. The obvious objection to such an approach is that it ignores all the other sacramental and nonsacramental dimensions of pastoral care. Neither does it necessarily reveal the implicit theologies present in the penitential praxis.

To this point we have been discussing complementary aspects of initiation and penance that are implicit in any theology and praxis of pastoral care. In chapter 1 we saw how the catechumenal model implements the biblical demand: turn to the Lord! Both the mission of the community that receives catechumens and the commitment demands to be made on these individuals are spelled out in the catechumenal process. Ideally, the first experience of pastoral care would be encountered in the catechumenate, or at least in a community that renews its already-initiated members by a similar process.

Here in chapter 2 we have been describing a similar process—the penitential process. As the pastoral care of the early church tried to call forth the charisms and ministries of the baptized, the problem of sin and the need for continuing conversion became evident. The penitential systems were, in effect, prolongations of the catechumenal process. They addressed the communal and personal dimensions of sin. Exclusion from the Eucharist, as the ultimate form of excommunication, only emphasized the ecclesial and catechumenal nature of such penance.[28]

When the praxis of penance in any particular historical period is discussed, the operative definitions of pastoral care for that period are uncovered—as in the case of the catechumenal process, our true understandings of salvation, church, sin, and mission are revealed as we turn (or refuse to turn) once more to God. At the same time theological priorities of pastoral care in that same historical period are also discovered. Cyprian's controversy with confessors of the faith, for example, over how penitents were to be received back into the community underlines and illustrates his ecclesiology and how pastoral care was shaped by that theology.

In our brief overview of the development of pastoral office and jurisdiction and its special focus in the praxis of penance, some corollaries for a theology of pastoral care emerge. First, at its best moments pastoral care, whatever form it may take, always tries to enable the Christian community to recommit itself to the work of the gospel. This sense of recommitment to mission is a test of continuing conversion on every level of the community.

Second, when ministries in the Christian community become too narrow in their conception or praxis—due more to juridical influence than to the effort of discernment—pastoral care inevitably suffers from a comparable narrowing. On the other hand, in the thirteenth century, for example, the surprising and rapid growth of such mendicant nonclerical groups as the Franciscans renewed pastoral care by opening up the ministries of lay preaching and penitential praxis to larger groups of Christians. The official church of the time discerned and encouraged these charisms.

Third, pastoral care may unwittingly encourage privatized notions of salvation and church if it does not renew the sense of mission and service in the individual Christian. This might explain in part why the new rituals of penance in our day do not seem to have succeeded in renewing the praxis of penance. Although the theology of a church in conversion is admirably expounded in the text of the 1973 rite (par. 9),[29] the praxis of the sacrament seems generally to perpetuate some of the very problems we have been discussing: Should every priest be given faculties for the sacrament of penance? To what extent can other ministries help prepare the penitent and the community for the sacramental expression of penance? How should the honest and fruitful reception of penance and reconciliation in the church evoke renewal and deepened service from both the community and the individual Christian?

Nearer the work biblically than the juridical definition of pastoral care cited above from Antoninus may be the seventh-century Irish sacramentary definition of priesthood: "Priesthood, if rightly and out of the love for the Lord accepted, must not be thought of as domination but as service, and submission rather than power."[30] In contemporary terms initiation and penance might suggest this new definition: pastoral care is the continuing effort to assist Christian communities and their members to deepen their baptismal commitment and penitential recommitment so that they may do the work of the gospel in our time.

From an ecumenical viewpoint the discussion of penance within a pastoral care context differs markedly from the polemical discussions of the sixteenth century. At its best moments pastoral care in all Christian churches has helped communities and individuals renew their sense of gospel-purpose. Although some Christian churches have not exercised this care as a sacramental ministry, there has been in all the Christian traditions a shared concern about ongoing conversion.

Once again some questions are suggested by the converging pastoral care experience of all the churches: To what extent can the Roman Catholic community learn from the early colonial Protestant churches that emphasized the narration of conversion experiences for building up of the whole community? In turn, does the contemporary Protestant community see a value, as did Luther, in symbolizing the communal and individual dimensions of penance?

## CHAPTER 3

# The *Medicus* Symbol
# of
# Pastoral Care

In Leonard Bernstein's *Mass,* the celebrant challenges his congrega-
tion: "What is there about me that you've been respecting and what
have you all been expecting to see?" Tearing off his vestments, he
adds: "Put it on, and you'll see: any one of you can be any one of me."
Bernstein has indeed dramatized both the ·high personal cost of
pastoral care and, often enough, the community's and its ministers'
narrow definitions of that care.

I have to this point purposely avoided giving a complete definition
of pastoral care. In chapter 1 some of the components of such a
definition were discussed: professional aspects of care and their
theological implications, and the catechumenate as a theological
model of that care. In chapter 2 some of the historical models of
pastoral care and their evolution were analyzed. Both chapters
pointed out the difficulty of delineating what pastoral care should be.

One of the best ways to arrive at a contemporary description of
pastoral care is to begin with a symbol that sums up the traditions of
pastoral care and suggests future developments. Inspired by its
scriptural roots, the Christian church has consistently employed the
Latin term *medicus* (meaning "doctor or healer") to describe the
pastoral work of Christ, and, by extension, that of his ministers. Paul
Ricoeur has argued that symbols should move us to thought. The
*medicus* symbol is a rich source for the rethinking of pastoral care
today.

As we trace the evolution of the term *medicus* from a scriptural
metaphor of Christ's salvific work to a general patristic term for
pastoral care, and on to a more juridical and limited understanding
of pastoral care, we begin to see some of the difficulties involved in a
*medicus*-based definition of such care. The key to the problem is the
use of the term *medicus* in current praxis. Once more, as in chapter 1,

the professional and the catechumenal models can assist us in translating *medicus* into the pastoral language of our own time.

The test of this contemporary translation of *medicus* will be the case proposed in chapter 1. The tension apparent in the praxis of Holy Cross Hospital's pastoral care arose not because of the professional character of the team ministry but in consequence of uncertainty about what *medicus* should mean in a specific pastoral care situation, whether or not the particular team member is ordained.

## CHRIST AS *MEDICUS*

Once a biblical connection is made between sin and sickness, a number of corollaries emerge. The first insight is that God is the healer or doctor: "I, the Lord, am your healer" (Exod. 15:26). Even the Jewish physician sees God as a true healer: "You are the true physician and your healing is true" (prayer at bloodletting).[1]

Because the Old Testament does not separate body and soul, connections between sin and sickness and between forgiveness and health are more easily made. It is not surprising that "healing" could become a technical term to picture God's unearned and saving action in the lives of his people. Healing in the Bible has as its purpose to enable conversion and to symbolize forgiveness.[2]

The twofold culmination of these developments is found in the Book of Isaiah. In chapter 53 the suffering servant is pictured as wounded for our sake so that we might be healed. In chapter 35 an eschatological vision of God's salvation is imaged through the transformation of sick people into healthy people: "Strengthen the hands that are feeble, make firm the knees that are weak, Say to those whose hearts are frightened: Be strong, fear not! . . . Then will the eyes of the blind be opened, the ears of the deaf be cleared; Then will the lame leap like a stag, then the tongue of the dumb will sing" (Isa. 35:3–6[a]).

In brief, God is indeed "healer/doctor" and healing is a privileged image of his salvation. When Jesus is described in the New Testament as one who heals, his messianic power and its salvific implications are already familiar ideas from the Old Testament. Even the use of the verb "to save" in reference to the whole person has Old Testament precedents.

All of these biblical traditions can be seen in condensed form in an early miracle story of Mark. In chapter 2 Mark tells of the healing of a paralytic. There is a familiar formula behind the story: (1) Jesus does a revolutionary action (forgiving sins), (2) the Pharisees object ("Who can forgive sins except God alone?"), (3) Jesus gives a definitive reply.[3] He answers: "People who are healthy do not need a doctor; sick people do. I have come to call sinners, not the self-righteous" (Mark 2:17/Matt. 9:12–13/Luke 5:31–32).

Jesus gives this answer after he has cured the paralytic and while he is eating with sinners. In this particular context Jesus is the messianic host,[4] who cures as proof of forgiveness and invites sinners to a festive meal. Once again it is the Old Testament images that have prepared us for Mark's story: "The lost I will seek out, the strayed I will bring back, the injured I will bind up, the sick I will heal" (Ezek. 34:16).

"People who are healthy do not need a doctor"—this proverbial saying sets up the now-familiar antitheses of healthy and sick, upright and sinner. In Mark's story the paralytic moves from sickness/sin to health/forgiveness.[5] The strong implication of the story is that Jesus is the doctor. Origen's commentary on this saying is but one example of how the early church favored this medical image of Jesus:

> So much for ordinary physicians. Now look at Jesus the heavenly physician. Come inside his room of healing, the church. Here comes a woman unclean from childbirth, a leper expelled from the camp owing to his unclean disease; and because this Jesus the physician is also the Word of God, he applies, not the juices of herbs, but the sacraments of the Word to their diseases.[6]

The symbol of Jesus as *medicus* is framed very carefully. The traditional Old Testament themes of God's care for the blind and the crippled have been transposed into the New Testament image of that same care now enfleshed in Jesus, the healer/doctor. When John Groppius, a German theologian at the Council of Trent, cites this *medicus* saying (Matt. 9:12) fifteen hundred years later, his interpretation is narrower than that of Origen: "Therefore, confession is necessary because sinners, having done badly, need indeed a doctor in order to be cured."[7] By the time of Trent the image clearly has other, more juridical meanings, as we shall see.

In addition to the *medicus* image, the scriptural episodes of the cleansing of the lepers (for example, Num. 12:9–15; 2 Kings 5:1–14; Matt. 8:2–4) and the raising of Lazarus are already favorite spots for patristic commentators to refer to forgiveness. Just as the cleansed lepers had to show themselves to the priest, so the sinner must come before the priest.[8] Just as Christ loosed Lazarus from the bonds of death, so the priest looses the bonds of the sinner (Matt. 16:19).[9]

As we read the medieval commentaries on the same passages, we detect a modulation in theme. These later commentators compare the healing not with canonical penance (as did Jerome, Gregory, and others) but with tariff penance as practiced in the twelfth century. The emphasis is now on the obligation to confess to a priest. It is the Lord who cures and raises to life, but it is the priest who verifies and declares these works of forgiveness.[10] This emphasis will reappear at the Council of Trent.[11]

These variations on the biblical themes of doctor and of curing and raising are a rich source of reflection for any theology of pastoral care. The church of Mark's time saw the messianic dimension of Christ's work of conversion and forgiveness, and concretized that perception in evocative images of his care for others. These same images became associated with the pastoral ministry of reconciliation in the early and medieval church, but what can easily be overlooked is the biblical reminder of God's unearned action.

All pastoral care is premised on what God alone initiates (justification). In other words God's care, as exemplified in Christ, is shown by the fact that he loved us first (1 John 4:10). This healing forgiveness remains a gratuitous gift. When the commentators began in an allegorical way to apply these biblical images of God's care to the specific problems of ongoing conversion and care, the original emphasis was sometimes lost.

## CHANGING IMAGES OF *MEDICUS*

In the twentieth century the word "doctor" has several connotations. In any given instance we know what it means by the way the word is used. In much the same way we can follow the church's expression of its pastoral care concerns in each historical period by the way in which it uses the *medicus* symbol.

As early as Ignatius of Antioch (c. 110) the biblical image is employed: "There is only one spiritual and corporal doctor" (Letter to the Ephesians 7:1–2). Somewhat later Cyril of Jerusalem describes the pastoral care of Christ as "curing the blind of body, and bringing light to minds; healing those lame and guiding visibly the steps of sinners to repentance. . . . Therefore, if anyone is sick in soul because of sin, he has a physician."[12] Once this general image has currency, then the sacraments are also described in medical terms.[13]

The ministers of the church are likewise described in terms of the same imagery. The *Apostolic Constitutions* provide us with an extended example: "Heal, O bishop, like a compassionate physician, all who have sinned, and employ methods that promote saving health. Do not confine yourself to cutting or cauterizing . . . but employ bandages . . . use mild and healing drugs, and sprinkle words of comfort as a soothing balm."[14]

As Adolf von Harnack and others have shown, the cult of the pagan god-doctor Aesculapius evoked a sharp reaction from Christianity. The result was not only development of the biblical metaphor of Christ as doctor, but also implementation of the meaning of the metaphor in practical ways. Christianity "did more than set up the actual Jesus against the imaginary Aesculapius of dreamland. Deliberately and consciously it assumed the form of the religion of salvation or healing . . . and at the same time it recognized that one of its chief duties was to care assiduously for the sick in body."[15]

By the time Augustine of Hippo started to make extensive use of the *medicus* image, it had already become a staple in discussions of sin, conversion, forgiveness, and specific problems of pastoral care.[16] In a beautiful phrase Augustine sums up this rich tradition which he has received: Christ is "the complete physician of our wounds."[17] Whether Augustine is speaking here of the way Christ treats Peter's denial ("He took the pulse of his [Peter's] heart")[18] or the way Christ treats our sins, it is striking how apt this image of pastoral care remains.[19]

## TRENT'S DOCTOR-JUDGE

An overriding image and ideal of pastoral care, then, has been that of Christ the doctor. By the sixth century we find the *medicus* analogy applied to the minister of penance in the somewhat different context of tax penance. As doctors must prescribe treatment according to the nature of the illness, so must the priest treat each penitent according to his or her situation.

But the analogy is further extended to include the juridical element that became prominent with tax penance. Alcuin (804) argues:

> The help a doctor may give is useless if the patient's wounds are not known to him. . . . Why did Christ command the lepers whom he had just cured to show themselves to the priest? Why did he ask others to loose Lazarus dead and resurrected by him after three days in the tomb? . . . It is a form of pride to disdain the priest as judge. . . . "Confess your faults to one another." . . . What does the "to one another" mean if not one person to another, *the guilty to the judge, the sick to the doctor?*[20]

As canon law comes to exert an increasing influence over pastoral and sacramental praxis and theory (recall Antoninus's definition of pastoral care in our discussion of power in chapter 2) the way is prepared for the Council of Trent's explanation of the priest as judge in terms of the more traditional doctor image: penance is not so much vindictive as medicinal, as all the Fathers felt. Thus, the Lateran Council says: "by a skilled doctor's practice. . . . *For God as judge punishes and as a father corrects; when he afflicts as a doctor he treats.*"[21]

In Trent's terminology the confessor is a doctor of souls.[22] But the analogy is then used to explain why integrity of confession (species and number of serious sins) is necessary: "For if a sick person is ashamed to lay bare his wound to the physician, no amount of medical skill will cure what it does not know. It follows, moreover, that even these circumstances which change the species of the sin are to be put forward in confession."[23] This is why the confessor is a judge, and absolution a juridical act. Just as wounds must be revealed before a prescription is given, so sins must be uncovered before sentence is given.[24]

The Roman Ritual which implemented the liturgical changes resulting from Trent's theological position sums up the uneasy connection between the judge metaphor and the doctor metaphor: "In the first place, the confessor should remember that he is to comport himself equally as a judge and doctor, established by God as a minister both of divine justice and mercy, as an arbiter between God and people."[25] Thus, some fifteen hundred years after the Christian church began to employ the *medicus* metaphor, it was still being used at Trent to describe the ministry of reconciliation.

But the use of the doctor analogy to explain the juridical nature of the sacrament of penance also reflects another development in the praxis and theory of pastoral care. There is at Trent a deep concern for pastoral care, but the discussions are complicated by the canonical models of ministry, and by the lack of a relevant liturgy to minister to people.[26]

Even this cursory history of the *medicus* image of pastoral care should make those of us who are involved in twentieth-century pastoral care pause to consider our own praxis. It is easy enough to see the theological limitations of the image when applied to pastoral care. Christ as doctor can too easily be understood in self-serving and nonecclesial ways. Salvation may then be defined in privatized terms that have nothing to do with a sense of mission to the world.

But just as we may wonder whether—or to what extent—this doctor image reflected actual praxis or only the theory of pastoral care in the third or tenth centuries, so today must we question our own images of the healing that pastoral care purports to bring. In more positive terms, how do we in our day bridge the chasm between the ideal of healing and its praxis? If we were to compile an honor roll of great doctors in pastoral care over the centuries, we might well begin by mentioning such names as Ignatius of Antioch, Cyprian of Carthage, Ambrose of Milan, Augustine of Hippo, Martin of Tours, and Caesar of Arles. What we can easily forget in listing these great healers is that they lived in very different pastoral situations from one another even within the same era or country. Each one had to translate the image of Christ the doctor for the praxis of his own time and situation. This remains the task of those who are involved in pastoral care today.

## THE CONTEMPORARY *MEDICUS*

Although much has been published in the way of theoretical material on the subject of the medical or psychological healer, each of us in praxis has had our own particular experiences—both good and bad—with the healing professions. Whatever the theoretical discussions may say about the professional criteria and training of medical practitioners, individually we cannot forget those effective doctors whom we have known and to whom we are lastingly grateful. In much the same way any theory of pastoral care will be challenged by the experience we have had personally with those who ministered to us with varying degrees of skill. Praxis does not contradict theory, but it does demand realistic assessment of what is actually being done.

Professional models of ministry are an attempt to wed the theoretical and practical dimensions of a certain type of work, such as that of a doctor or of a Christian minister of the gospel. Any professional model, as we noted already in chapter 1, involves not only specialized training but also peer control and accountability; it includes not only the task to be performed but also the values implied in the role. In the case of pastoral care the professional model attempts to spell out the conditions for successful implementation of the *medicus* vision that we have been discussing.

While no one denies the values that professionalism inculcates, some theologians fear that it carries with it the danger of reducing ministry to a single role or function. Pastoral care, for example, might be reduced simply to a counseling role, or to the role of expert on human relations. But to embrace such a role limitation would be to forget the theological underpinnings of the *medicus* model. The late Urban T. Holmes, reacting to such reduced descriptions of ministry, suggested metaphors such as shaman, mana-person, clown, storyteller, and wagon master to illustrate the complexity of God's work and our share in it.[27]

We need to understand the professional model of ministry as including both the personal qualities and the wide-ranging knowledge and skills that prepare a person to do the specialized work of the gospel within the various structures of the Christian community. Such an understanding helps us to regard pastoral care in more realistic terms. While in no way reducing pastoral care simply to a helping role, it keeps before us the practical issues involved both in training Christians for this ministry and in building a theology of pastoral care. In fact such an approach assumes the traditional belief that "doing the truth" and "saying the truth" are complementary activities of practical theology.[28]

*Ministry in America,* the recent study of five thousand respondents in forty-seven denominations to which we referred in chapter 1, provides an interesting view of the contemporary understanding of the *medicus.* Eleven major themes were selected to test readiness for ministry. Although these themes are part of a general model of ministry, all refer directly or indirectly to a conception of *medicus* and pastoral care.[29]

These eleven ministerial themes can be broken down into two basic groups: those that seem to reflect purely professional models, and those that have an explicit theological component.[30]

Such themes as an "open, affirming style," "caring for persons under stress," "congregational leadership" (that is, "administrative style . . . that is efficient, and that properly utilizes conflict"), and their negative counterparts fall under the purely professional themes. "Theologian in life and thought" (that is, "broad general knowledge and theological understanding and conscious examination of the minister's own life"), "ministry from a personal commitment of faith," "development of fellowship and worship," "ministry to community and world," "priestly-sacramental ministry" are examples of themes with a theological component.

All these themes obviously represent a composite of praxis and theory. They represent a search for and ideals about what a caring ministry should be. Themes in the first group deal with both the personal qualities of the minister and the relationship between the minister and the community. To examine these professional themes I will use here the three theological criteria proposed already in chapter 1 in connection with temptations related to the professional model: conversion, commitment, and transcendence.

## Conversion

Conversion is never an abstract experience. It is always the result of and accompaniment to a pastoral care that is initiated by God and facilitated through the ministry of other persons. In other words, the ways in which God heals us (justification) are enfleshed in the lives of specific persons and communities. But we cannot separate God's care for us from his invitation to care for others. "Conversion," then, is ultimately a theological description of God's praxis— his continuing and enabling care.

The professional qualities of individual ministers should be equal to those of their secular counterparts. Prospective therapists and counselors, for example, are usually encouraged to seek therapeutic help to the extent that it is needed. Therapists are not expected to be perfectly congruent, but their willingness to deal with their incongruities is regarded as a sign of professional readiness.

Yet ever since the Donatist controversy of the fifth century, in which the Donatists insisted on the holiness of the minister as essential for "valid" sacraments, there has been a tendency to emphasize the objective nature of ministry to the detriment of the related subjective question, namely, the ability of *this minister* to minister. Augustine, in response to the Donatists, rightly defended God's gratuitous action in the sacramental ministry of the church. What is sometimes forgotten is Augustine's insistence on personal credibility in the life of the minister, and the gospel praxis he fostered among his own priests at Hippo.

Within the Roman Catholic church, with its tradition of a strong sacramental dimension in pastoral care, there is always the danger that the subjective aspects of ministry may be minimized in the name of preserving the objective and gratuitous nature of God's action. This is the other extreme from a professionalism cloaked in a religious garb. The problem is reflected in an intervention made at Trent on November 12, 1547, by a theologian reacting to the use of the *medicus* metaphor in relation to the sacrament of penance. He supported his theological position by arguing that "even bad spiritual doctors can absolve."[31] But such an assertion, to say the least, begs the question and results in pastoral minimalism.

Professional skills and accountability are certainly needed if we are ever to get past minimal definitions of ministry and pastoral care. In fact, professional models propose levels of expected competence and congruence that can facilitate ministry. In 1972, for example, Douglas T. Hall and Benjamin Schneider published a fine study, *Organizational Climates and Careers: The Work Lives of Priests*,[32] in which the professional lives of priests were examined with the help of a psychological model of success and failure. In an earlier study, *The American Bishops' Report on the Priesthood*,[33] psychosocial analyses of certain dimensions of ordained ministry were made in order to clarify, in part, some of the problems inherent in professional training of seminarians and reeducation of priests. Such studies and the models they employ are an immense help in improving the work of pastoral care.

But when conversion is an active measure of our ministry, we are pushed past the respectable limits that a professional model sets for itself. In brief, to be empathetic and unconditionally accepting according to models of the American Psychological Association is a good beginning for those in pastoral care, but conversion deals with deeper wounds and wider horizons than any therapeutic model envisioned by Carl Rogers or any sociological model of Talcott Parsons. Conversion requires more demanding tasks of pastoral care because it defines what *medicus* must mean for individuals and communities in the contexts of their experience and times, and in view of what the kingdom of God entails.

## Commitment

The professional and personal qualities of those who work in pastoral care must also be measured in terms of a second theological criterion—that of commitment to the work of the gospel and the mission of the church in this world. The term *medicus* sums up the healing that is received and given to a person in a particular stage of life. The professional and personal qualities of the minister— "positive," "flexible," "empathetic," "leader"—are in a sense attempts at describing the results of a dynamic and staged process of painful change, continuing growth, and deepening commitment. Some of the thematic data in the *Ministry in America* study are expressions of professional commitment: "behaves responsibly," "informed counseling skills . . . made readily available," "shared leadership."

A theological critique, while including such descriptions of professional standards, must demand much more in the way of religious commitment. Pastoral care, after all, is ultimately judged by its efforts to enable and to evoke deeper commitment to God's work and his church's mission. Christ the *medicus* is described in Christian tradition, as we have seen, in terms of his care for and commitment to his people. Pastoral care ministers in turn will never be perfect models of commitment, anymore than are the people they serve, but God does enable both those cared for and their ministers to deepen the ways in which they direct their human energies and resources for the sake of others.

When we think of Christian commitment, names rather than ideas suggest themselves. The names of Paul of Tarsus and Dom Helder Camara of Brazil, Augustine of Hippo and Mother Teresa of Calcutta, Francis of Assisi and Dorothy Day flesh out the otherwise abstract notion of commitment. Within our own experience we instinctively remember the names of people whom we associate with commitment—a devoted parent, a selfless teacher, an affirming friend. If we analyze the lives of such people, we begin to understand and appreciate the core meaning of the word "commitment" as expressed already in its Latin root: "to go/send with." Committed people enable and evoke commitment from others by the ways in which they themselves walk "with" others through the crises of their lives, giving them courage to draw new meaning and purpose from the burdens and trials.[34]

The Christian facing major surgery or bereavement, or trying to deal with an alcoholic or drug-dependent family member, generally perceives crisis as an event or situation demanding resources that he or she does not seem to have. One experiences the crisis as painful because of one's apparent incapacity to give or do what is needed, or because the situation is out of one's control. Pastoral care is always dealing with crises of one sort or another. But it is easy for the minister of pastoral care to forget the purpose of such crises. As a result the pastoral minister may pursue the short-term goal of helping a person, while forgetting the long-term goal of calling that person to a new sense of purpose and service in life.

Recent research has confirmed the earlier insights of Erik Erikson and others that each life-stage demands of us new tasks and commitments. The crises that follow upon such demands force us to reassess the richness of our gifts and to stretch ourselves to meet the requirements of the new situation. In other words the positive result of a crisis that is honestly worked through is the appropriation of strengths and responsibilities that prepare us to live out our current life-stage with new vigor and purpose.

But this process of disorientation and reorientation, of crisis and recommitment, is not simply a secular footnote in the religious autobiography of the Christian. Conflicts honestly dealt with in our stories reveal rather the limited self-definitions we have too easily lived with, and the new resources and the new gifts of self that are possible in our current stage of life.

Commitment to God's kingdom is a result of this recurring process. Erikson's definition of change is also an accurate theological description of conversion: "True change is a matter of worthwhile conflict for it leads through the painful consciousness of one's position to a new conscience in that position."[35] A "new conscience," however, can only be defined in terms of commitment to the values and priorities of God's kingdom.

### Transcendence

A third critique of any set of professional themes about pastoral care ministry must involve reference to transcendence. When we are open to the ultimate direction and meaning of our experience— God—then we have begun to experience self-transcendence. Another way of stating this, perhaps, is to say that for the Christian there is no such thing as secular experience. Both conversion and commitment are linked to self-transcendence.

If, as Charles Winquist has recently suggested, the minister must be able not only to speak forcefully of experience but also to help us appropriate that experience, then the minister too must be open to the experience of self-transcendence.[36] Such transcendence enables the minister to celebrate the symbols of God's presence and our response with greater credibility and honesty. Such awareness of God's action in our lives makes his objective presence among us believable because of our own genuine subjectivity.

To sum up, the *medicus* tradition is translated into the concerns of our age, in part, by the current professional demands made on all the healing disciplines. But the theological criteria of conversion, commitment, and transcendence also give depth and direction to such professional demands. In fact, these gospel tests of the authentic *medicus* reflect the invitation that both the Fathers of the church and the Council of Trent like to comment on: "Doctor, heal yourself."

### THE ECCLESIAL CONTEXT
### OF MINISTRY

The second set of themes in *Ministry in America* reflects specifically theological concerns with respect to the minister's own faith situation and the relation of the minister to the Christian community. To critique this second set of themes—"theologian in life and thought," "ministry from a personal commitment to faith," "development of fellowship and worship," "ministry to community and world"—I will once again employ the criteria of conversion, commitment, and transcendence, this time, however, telescoped together in their underlying concern, namely, the ecclesial context of ministry.

By definition the *medicus* is someone involved with human pain. But there is always the professional and religious temptation to evade our own wounds while dealing expertly with those of others.

The faculty of any graduate professional school is familiar with the problem of getting students to answer questions that they prefer to pose only to others. In theological faculties, for example, students preparing to work in pastoral care ministries often tend to absorb their course material from a one-dimensional, academic viewpoint without facing up to the questions implicitly posed about their own experience of faith and motivation for ministry.

This second set of major themes from the *Ministry in America* study is important, then, because the themes are forceful theological reminders of the privileged role of the minister in symbolizing and proclaiming what God as *medicus* is doing among us. This privileged service derives not from the merits of the minister but from the nature of God's gratuitous action in our midst, which precedes our experience of it. Understanding the pastoral care minister in this sense as symbolizer, not simply ritualizer, helps us to avoid both the one-sided notion of objective ministry—a pastoral care that refuses to deal with the personal stance of the minister—and the functional notion of pastoral care that concentrates exclusively on the services rendered.

Paul takes up these same concerns at the point where he gives his own description of God as *medicus:* "God, in Christ, was reconciling the world to himself, not counting [people's] transgressions against them, and . . . he . . . entrusted the message of reconciliation to us. This makes us ambassadors for Christ, God as it were appealing through us" (2 Cor. 5:19–20). Paul maintains that when he, Paul, preaches, God is actually the speaker. C. K. Barrett in commenting on the Pauline assertion says: "Where Paul is at work, Christ whom he represents is at work."[37]

In other words, an important development of the *medicus* tradition is based on the insight that the minister can symbolize only out of his or her own experience. Thanks to the seminal work of Ricoeur on symbol, we appreciate more keenly the multiple and inexhaustible intentions of each symbol,[38] and how symbol gathers the many strands of our experience. What we must immediately add, however, is that the meaning of our shared experience is always found in the context of our acknowledged and unacknowledged communities. As Bernard Lonergan reminds us, "Community is not just an aggregate of individuals within a frontier, for that overlooks its formal constituent, which is *common meaning.* Such common meaning calls for a *common field of experience* and when that is lacking, *people get out of touch.*"[39]

Intimately linked to the personal experience of the pastoral minister and to the whole pastoral care enterprise, as we noted in our discussion of Vatican II in chapter 1, are the implicit and explicit connections we make between our own personal meanings and common meanings, between our own personal experience and that of the church. If, as argued in chapter 1, pastoral care is measured, in part, by the ecclesial awareness of mission and the service it evokes from the community, then the meanings we think we hold in common must be critically reexamined in each Christian age. Doctrinal uniformity does not in and of itself assure the common meanings that can constantly forge and reform the church. Rather it is the *medicus* tradition which reminds us of the deeper wounds to which pastoral care must attend: insular definitions of salvation, a selective sense of service, operative theologies that excuse us from a sense of social justice and public witness, self-serving celebration and reception of the sacraments such as seem to excuse us from the underlying demands of the Word of God. When pastoral care has successfully called the local and universal Christian community to embrace common meanings, then the promise of gospel-healing has once more been revealed in its true richness.

## THE CATECHUMENATE AS
## *MEDICUS* PROCESS

In chapter 1 I suggested the catechumenate as a model of pastoral care. The catechumenate was and is first and foremost the praxis of Christian living. In the deepest sense of the word, the catechumenate helped Christians to be "professional," that is, "to profess or proclaim what God in Christ was doing in the midst of his people." Because of the very nature of the process, Christians learned praxis definitions of realities that for some people remain only words: "church," "grace," "salvation," "mission."

Here at the end of this sketch of the *medicus* tradition another characteristic of the catechumenate should now be obvious: the catechumenate implemented the *medicus* model by healing sinners so that they could become servants of the gospel. If a second-century catechumen in Rome or Carthage were asked how the catechumenate healed, the answer might go something like this: "The gospel-word has taught me to serve and not be served. To learn this, I had to turn away from a life style and a set of values that were self-centered. I could not have done this without the example and support of this Christian community. By the way they cared for me, they taught me to care for others. By their care, I was enabled to be committed."

In a long and famous chapter on "The Gospel of Love and Charity" in his classic work *The Mission and Expansion of Christianity in the First Three Centuries,* Harnack implicitly paid tribute to the success of the catechumenate as the praxis of healing sinners for service. He finds no better way to sum up this *medicus* practice than by repeating Tertullian's famous boast: "It is our care for the helpless, our practice of loving kindness, that brands us in the eyes of many of our opponents."[40]

Realistically, however, the catechumenate seems to have been successful only in the earlier centuries of the church's existence, when commitment demands were high and motivation fairly clear. This should give us pause as we try to restore the catechumenate in this latter part of the twentieth century. To set up a series of ritual times and spaces is not necessarily to restore the catechumenate. If the catechumenal preparation of candidates for Christian initiation is to be effective, then real healing and care for the wounds of radical sin as well as individual sins must be given. This would be the *medicus* symbol in praxis. Anything less than this would be to mislead the prospective or returning Christian with respect to the meaning of Paul's baptismal teaching: as Christ, so we. It would be to fill the Christian communities, as did some of the fourth-century catechumenates, with an ambiguously motivated people.

There seem to be some parallel lessons here for both the praxis and theology of pastoral care. Ten or twenty years ago the pastoral care movement appeared to be in danger of equating psychological congruence with Christian healing in both praxis and theory. Increasingly, though, we are beginning to see that psychological and Christian definitions of healing actually differ in their ultimate extension and purpose. A commitment to gospel values accepts but surpasses humanistic congruence, and sees the kingdom of God as the final test of present tasks and future hopes.

Pastoral care, understood as another form of the catechumenate, is a process of healing the Christian community and its individual members so that they might take up the work of the gospel. It is the fruit of true penance and conversion, such as we discussed in chapter 2. Like the catechumenate, pastoral care in its various forms must clarify the experience and values of Christian men and women if these persons are to become more honest and accountable in sharing the healing they have received. If such descriptions of pastoral care are accepted, then another catechumenal corollary follows: pastoral care scrutinizes and clarifies the real praxis of the local Christian community as well as that of its individual members.

## CHAPTER 4

# Praxis and Theology
# in
# Pastoral Care

For sixteenth-century Christians pastoral care was symbolized by Charles Borromeo, the archbishop of Milan who cared for his plague-ridden people. In the nineteenth century John Vianney, pastor of a rural French parish, or Father Damien of Molokai, protector of lepers, may have epitomized pastoral care. In the twentieth century Father Flanagan of Boy's Town or Dorothy Day of *The Catholic Worker* or Mother Teresa of Calcutta probably exemplify the meaning of pastoral care in its many forms. Pastoral care, in other words, cannot be limited to particular kinds of work or to certain exclusive ministries. It is as broad as the redemptive need of the world in which the ministers of such care find themselves.

As a rule charismatic figures in pastoral care do not start out with theories on the subject or advanced training in the field. They simply respond to the specific situations of their times, motivated by Jesus' reminder, "As often as you did it for one of my least brothers" (Matt. 25:40). Technically speaking, then, pastoral care is, in the first instance, praxis: a way of doing, caring, and being with others in the name of and for the sake of Christ. This praxis of pastoral care, however, does not spontaneously happen. It is the result of effort. A major task of the Christian community has always been that of teaching us to care.

In chapter 1 the catechumenal model was proposed as a praxis model of pastoral care. Ideally both candidates and the initiated help one another—by a shared formation and renewal in Christian values and service—to understand the Pauline admonition to be "as Christ."

Chapter 2 continued this theme in another key. Because perfect Christians do not abound in any century, penance and reconciliation as an extension of the catechumenal model has always been a part of pastoral care. If we, as community and as individuals, were not constantly being called to penance, pastoral care would be reduced to a bureaucratic form of churchly social services.

The *medicus* figure of chapter 3 can be regarded in each Christian age as an ideal in search of a praxis. We saw how the Christian church sometimes limited its praxis of pastoral care because of more juridical notions about the *medicus*.

## THE THEOLOGICAL CONCERN

In this chapter our concern is with the theology of pastoral care. The major contribution of such a theology should be to clarify the actual praxis of pastoral care. Theology is particularly apt for this task because it asks questions which help us evaluate the quality of pastoral care in our particular situation: What pastoral care tasks take up the majority of your time? Why are these pastoral care tasks more important than others? Does your pastoral care invite people to take more responsibility for the building up of the body of Christ? How does your pastoral care help people look forward to God's future kingdom and work for it now?

Behind each of these practical questions is a central theological teaching on the meaning of salvation, church, and God's kingdom. Such questions bring us back to the familiar scenes of our pastoral care ministries with new insight about our actual priorities and whether they stand up to the measure of God's meaning. Ultimately, theology asks those who care for God's people whether they are themselves spending their efforts on the right pastoral tasks and for the right reasons.

This chapter, then, is not a theory of pastoral care or—as it is called in schools of theology—a practical theology. Yet some practical lessons can be learned from the last four centuries of effort to train people for pastoral care by the scholarly discipline called practical theology. While this chapter will not discuss in great detail the current praxis-theory debates, we can learn something about our own particular praxis by examining the historical praxis of pastoral care in the North African church at the time of Cyprian and the time of Augustine. Finally, some theological criteria will be suggested for examining our own pastoral care praxis. Not only our pastoral ministries but theology itself should benefit from such criteria. Sound pastoral praxis has always recalled theology to its ultimate task—to make the proclamation of God's unearned love more accessible to the people of each generation.

## Communication and Common Meaning

A guiding insight for this chapter is Bernard Lonergan's reminder that pastoral theology is a question of communication. In outlining his theological method Lonergan posits eight specialties: research, interpretation, history, dialectic, foundations, doctrines, systematics, and communications. But in communications "theological reflection bears fruit."[1]

There is always the possibility of new unity among people when they can effectively communicate, and thus appropriate, the common meanings of the gospel message. Community itself, after all, is the result of such shared common meaning. Thus, for Lonergan, "the Christian church is the community that results from the outer communication of Christ's message and from the inner gift of God's love. Since God can be counted on to bestow his grace, practical theology is concerned with the effective communication of Christ's message."[2]

All effective pastoral care is a question of communication and common meaning. The very presence of pastoral care in the church is a reminder that we are still on *this* side of the kingdom of God, we are here where divided communities and only partially shared meanings are by no means a rare experience. Pastoral care must communicate not only on the feeling, intellectual, and ethical levels. It must also deal with the responsible decision-making process within which Christians appropriate the gospel meanings that unite them.

## Congruence and Communication

Before proceeding to the theological discussion of shared gospel meanings, the psychological dimension of this question needs to be treated at least briefly. When at the end of the previous chapter I mentioned the danger of equating psychological congruence with Christian conversion, the intention was not to detract from the important insights that the human sciences have contributed to the praxis and theory of pastoral care. In fact, the dichotomy that sometimes exists between theological theory and pastoral care praxis is the result, in part, of naive assumptions about such terms as communication and common meaning. The therapeutic process, on the contrary, has to deal with these abstract terms in the complicated situations and narrative of people's experience. Incongruence, after all, cannot be separated fom the inadequate contact people have with their own stories. In turn, common meanings cannot be appropriated apart from that same experience.

The way in which the therapeutic process confronts this problem of communication and commitment is, in significant ways, similar to the conversion process. Much of the misinterpretation and lack of appropriation of experience is caused by our unrealistic ideal self-images. Many of our autobiographical narratives can clash with these naive but powerful self-images. In other words, we hide from our experience if it contradicts the ideal of what we or others think we should be.

As therapists well know, poor communication and unappropriated meanings and commitments are often the result of this tension between our ideal selves and our real selves. The dynamic of healing rests, in part, on the ability of the therapist to afford the incongruent person "free space" within which new strength to confront and reinterpret personal experience is made possible. The therapist's empathetic acceptance enables a less-distorted form of communication with the other person. It can also provide, as family counseling demonstrates, a similar experience for larger groups.

A convincing indication of healing, in this process, is the growing ability and willingness of a person to appropriate values and meanings, and to make commitments. This is now possible because the congruent person is more securely rooted in his or her shared experience and as a result has a new perspective and energy to deal with the future by fully living the present.

Although there is a great deal of psychological theory, therapy—like pastoral care—is ultimately a question of praxis. Whether dealing with an individual or a group, there is always a question of distorted communication with self and others. The therapist, in turn, must be able to provide the acceptance and openness that can permit change and insight in the incongruent person.

The use of psychological models in pastoral care has provoked a reevaluation not only because of the professional standards proposed, but also to challenge simplistic definitions of communication and common meaning. Even from such a cursory review of the healing process, the question emerges, Does pastoral care in praxis have as demanding a definition of the conversion process with its corollaries of communication and common meaning?

Once again a brief historical survey, this time of some important eighteenth- and nineteenth-century debates on the nature of practical theology, can serve to preface and focus the discussion.

## The Triumph of Functionalism

After the sixteenth-century Council of Trent pastoral care was shaped to a great extent by seminaries and the pastoral formation they gave to future priests. There was an attempt to draw out the pastoral corollaries of the various theological disciplines. Unfortunately, casuistic or juridical interpretations of sacramental theology by moral theology and canon law were frequent. The pastoral result was often a split between the religious meanings and priorities of the institutional church and those of its people, between an official worship and folk piety. The same ministry of visiting the sick or of hearing confession, for example, could be interpreted in different ways by the ministering priest and by the lay person. Such pastoral care could easily result in closer juridical bonding to the church but without any deepened commitment to the mission of the church. It could reenforce privatized notions of salvation without evoking new willingness to serve.

In the eighteenth century Franz S. Rautenstrauch, a Benedictine, proposed that pastoral theology be a required course in the Catholic faculties of theology in German universities. He saw in the professional preparation demanded by the law and medicine faculties of the universities a model for both the theoretical and practical education of priests. While the professional components of his model seem strikingly contemporary, there were also elements of clericalism and Jansenism attached to this approach.[3]

Johann M. Sailer was another influential eighteenth-century thinker on the question of pastoral care in Germany. "Pastoral wisdom" was the catch phrase that summarized his pastoral concerns. Sailer felt that the ideal pastor would combine a practical experience and a theoretical capacity so as to be able to critically analyze pastoral praxis. All theology must be considered as pastoral, he argued, and those formed by such theology must be motivated by a sense of personal service.[4] Praxis, in other words, was a central element of Sailer's plan. This was in contrast to other approaches, such as that of the Tübingen school of theology, which insisted that practical theology did not derive from but led to the praxis of pastoral care.[5]

By the middle of the nineteenth century, however, a new "functionalism" had developed. Practical theology came to be viewed as how-to-do-it pastoral care. In place of the emphasis on a theoretical analysis of the praxis situation, pastoral care was divided into a succession of specialties, such as liturgy, homiletics, and catechetics, to be taught. The danger in such a functional approach to pastoral care is always that one will lose sight of the ecclesial and eschatological purposes of such care; the concern for pastoral techniques can cloud over the need for the purpose of healing as such.[6] There is also the danger, as Norbert Mette points out, that pastoral authority and the canonization of certain pastoral procedures will receive greater attention than the gospel proclamation and mission which authentic pastoral care ought always to provide.[7]

My purpose here in briefly sketching some of these eighteenth- and nineteenth-century discussions concerning practical theology was to situate the problem of pastoral care praxis. The triumph of nineteenth-century functionalism in most European and American seminaries until Vatican II is a forceful reminder of how distorted the question of pastoral care praxis had actually become, despite the initially promising insights and educational innovations of Rautenstrauch, Sailer, and others. The success of the functional models of pastoral care training and theory reflect, in turn, theologies of juridical ecclesiology and privatized sacramental theology which remained unchallenged, for the most part, until the early decades of this century.

## THE RELATION BETWEEN
## THEORY AND PRAXIS

Praxis can be a deceptive term. For some people pastoral care praxis refers to the techniques used in hospital ministry, pastoral counseling, or catechetics. If such an understanding of praxis is accepted, then the theory derived will be equally superficial. In actuality praxis operates on several levels of meaning. The sacramental praxis of marriage, for example, mirrors accurately not only the social and psychological values of both the community and the couple, but also their operative theological understandings of church and mission. Further, praxis may not always be what it appears to be; unfamiliarity with the culture or personal background of the persons involved can lead to misinterpretations.

The late-twentieth-century retrieval of the catechumenal process might serve as an example of the relation between praxis and theory. If a visitor to a diocese where the catechumenate is in use were to ask the bishop, local priest, religious education director, and the catechumens themselves to describe the actual process of the catechumenate in a specific parish, that visitor might receive quite different praxis descriptions. Although theologically the theory of the catechumenate as a conversion process might be accepted by all, the local bishop or priest may in praxis employ the catechumenate only as a functional model replacing the older praxis of convert instructions. The catechumens' assessment of their experience might focus on the social or informational character of the catechumenate, or even stress the religious decisions it enabled them to make.

Although the theory of the catechumenate emphasizes the ecclesial nature of initiation, catechumenal praxis may thus give the lie to this view by the way in which the process is actually conducted. Though the theology of the catechumenate might underscore the sense of gospel-mission, the praxis of any particular catechumenate may cue its candidates only on institutional expectations, such as attendance at mass and "helping out."

In other words, not only are there different definitions of praxis, but theory and praxis with respect to the same experience may be quite disparate. In fact, pastoral care is a complex scene in which theory and praxis are so inextricably interwoven that it is difficult to assess what is really going on. If our pastoral care is truly to implement the gospel mandate to evangelize and proclaim what God is doing among us, then we must seek to clarify the relationship between theory and praxis. One major help in this task is to remember that theory provides an intellectual orientation while authentic praxis requires ongoing conversion.

## Critical Correlation

Matthew Lamb has extensively treated the different models of praxis and theory.[8] In the fifth of his models, which Lamb calls the model of critical correlation, Christian praxis is supposed to lead to theory in such a way that theory in turn reforms or corrects that praxis and enables a more authentic faith.[9] This dialectical process of praxis/theory/praxis is a form of communication in which we critically examine the actions of our lives and their shared meanings. But since our world and its praxis also tolerates systematic distortion of communication, it is all the more important for the Christian community to discern what is really happening in its praxis.[10] To be naive in interpreting our praxis is to run the risk of being dishonest in the symbols of our pastoral care. The shared meanings of gospel-living and pastoral care are always the first victims of such a situation.

One objection to the Lamb proposal needs to be faced. Does anyone ever develop a praxis without first having at least some implicit theories about it? What is the use, then, of insisting on the primacy of praxis, when we always come to our starting point with prior theories?

The fact is that we cannot analyze praxis as if it occurred in a vacuum. Whether we discuss counseling or ecclesial or sacramental aspects of pastoral care, we are from the outset always dealing with a mixed situation.

On the other hand, the striking thing about pastoral care praxis is how widely it can differ—for better or worse—from our most-cherished theories. Our theological formation in the theory of the sacrament of reconciliation or of the catechumenate, for example, may be quite sophisticated, reflecting a post–Vatican II mind, while our praxis in these same situations reveals a pre-Tridentine orientation.

## Hidden Ecclesiologies

Long before there were theories about church, there was a pastoral care praxis in each of the local congregations. And even where such praxis appears to be uniform among the churches, there are always features which reflect the particular people involved. The way in which a particular Christian community cares for its members reveals a great deal about its vision of "being church," and about the cost to such a church of its caring. A famous historical example involves the dispute between Stephen, bishop of Rome, and Cyprian, bishop of Carthage, in the mid–third century.

Cyprian had heard that Stephen, in receiving heretics back into the church, only imposed hands on them in reconciliation. As Cyprian reminds his Roman colleague, the African church would have rebaptized such heretics. Behind this praxis of the North African church, there is a theory of what church means. In effect, Cyprian is questioning not only Stephen's theology of initiation but, more important, his ecclesiology.

Cyprian rebaptizes heretical priests because he believes that they cannot otherwise confer valid sacraments. His reasoning is summed up in one line: "One who does not have the church as mother, cannot have God as Father."[11] Outside the church, argues Cyprian, there is neither the Spirit nor forgiveness. Persons outside the church cannot give what they do not possess. Therefore, heretics cannot give the sacrament of initiation into the church.

Though this theology of church sounds pastorally harsh and theologically inadequate to modern ears, it sprang no doubt from the commitment model that a church accustomed to persecution might follow. In any case when Cyprian reiterates the North African pastoral care praxis on this subject, he reveals his implicit model of the church and the nature of its pastoral care.

Stephen's church, on the other hand, is no stranger to persecution or to gospel commitment. When Stephen explains the theology behind the differing praxis of the Roman church with respect to heretics—the power of Christ's name renders even heretical baptism valid—this represents much more than an isolated theory about sacramental validity. In explaining the pastoral care of initiation in the Roman church, Stephen provides a challenging but somewhat different sense of what it means to "be church."

The resulting pastoral care of heretics is a pastoral corollary to the way in which the Roman Christian community is a church together. To notice only two opposing sacramental theories in this historical incident is to miss the praxis which gives a profile of two different Christian communities and the way in which they live out the gospel message.

The conflicting praxes of the Roman church and the North African church thus afford the occasion for clarifying the pastoral care of both communities. In each case, the community was forced to reflect on the theory behind its praxis and to articulate that theory. This led, in turn, to an eventual reevaluation of the praxis of the North African Christian community in dealing with repentant heretics. The pastoral care of that community became more compassionate as a result.

Under the apparent doctrinal and ritual uniformity of today's church we may easily forget that a closer look at pastoral praxis can disclose some surprising theories. An easy way to illustrate such theory-behind-the-praxis is to recall the sequel to the debate between Cyprian and Stephen. Augustine, an episcopal successor in the same North African church, finds himself some hundred and fifty years later confronting the heretical Donatists. The Donatists, in both praxis and theory, see room in the church only for the pure and holy. There is no place for sinners in their communities. The Donatists even cite Cyprian against Augustine to justify their praxis of rebaptizing or reordaining Christians who have received baptism or ordination from unworthy ministers.

What model of the church is implicit in the Donatist community? Obviously, the Donatists have forgotten that the church and its sacraments belong to Christ—they are his. As Augustine argues, "The sacraments are no less those of Christ and of the church because they are badly employed by heretics or the impious."[12]

Secondly, the Donatists' conception of church is an unrealistic one in praxis and in theory because conversion and commitment to the gospel are not seen as a lifetime effort. Unlike the Lord who eats with sinners, the Donatists will sit down only with the just.

Like Cyprian, Augustine uses the parable of the wheat and the tares which remain together until harvest time as a model for an imperfect church on its way to the kingdom. Augustine argues that the way in which the Donatists care for their members betrays a lack of awareness of a crucial pastoral distinction—the difference between sacraments only ritually celebrated and sacraments fruitfully appropriated. Augustine speaks of a communion of sacraments that should lead to a society of saints.

In other words, Augustine is no less insistent than Cyprian in his demand for Christian commitment. For Augustine, however, God's unearned initiative and compassion is the continuing foundation of the church in the face of our flawed commitment. This is a crucial insight for any praxis or theology of pastoral care. In the history of the Christian church each time this insight has been lost sight of, heretical forms of rigorism have been mistaken for gospel commitment.

To develop this insight about fruitful commitment to the gospel, Augustine again reviews the praxis of the church. He notices that it is the praxis of the church not to repeat the sacraments of initiation and orders. He reasons theologically that there must be some perduring quality about these celebrations that obviates any need for repetition. The technical word he uses to describe this quality is "character." The term was already rich in meaning as the stamping on a coin, and as the identifying sign born by soldiers and slaves.

Augustine extends this idea of character: "Our God and Lord Jesus Christ seeks the deserter, destroys the sin, but he does not obliterate his character."[13] Just as a military deserter always bears the external but ineradicable mark of the emperor, so the Christian always bears the mark of Christ that is sacramentally bestowed. Character is a consecration and commitment to the service of Christ. Augustine sees this symbolized consecration in both initiation and orders. Both sacraments are ways in which Christ enables the church to fulfill its mission.[14] The Donatists had missed this crucial point. Sacraments are given to us, not because of our merits, but because without them the church could not fulfill its mission. To speak of a perduring quality, or character, is a theological way of describing the praxis situation of a flawed but mission-bound church: proclamation of and witness to the gospel.

Our Christian praxis, then, bears watching. A simple comparison may summarize this discussion. The praxis of both Augustine's church and the medieval church was the same: initiation once given is never repeated. But in Augustine's praxis and theory the primary emphasis is on the ecclesial nature of the sacrament, which in turn leads to a definition of character as the continuing membership in Christ's community for our shame or glory. Among the scholastic theologians of the medieval period initiation is seen more in terms of the washing away of sins, which then leads to an understanding of character as a personal grace.[15] In brief, under an apparently uniform praxis there are actually two different praxes and theories. The fifth-century and the medieval praxes resulted in different priorities in pastoral care.

## THEOLOGY IN PRAXIS

The ultimate common meaning of the Christian community is the kingdom of God. In other words, whether we ask why the church exists or wherein salvation consists, the eschatological direction of all creation must influence our answer. When we question what pastoral care should be doing, our answer must be shaped by the priorities and concerns of God's future and its ramifications for our present. If we lose sight of the eschatological criterion, we risk a pastoral care praxis that may have little or nothing to do with God's plan for creation's future.

### The Eschatological Criterion

The praxis of pastoral care therefore must be constantly reevaluated in terms of its ultimate purpose—God's new creation. The problem with such a statement of the eschatological criterion is its apparent vagueness. By definition we have no definitive experience of God's kingdom. Of what practical pastoral use is it, then, to suggest such a norm?

The answer can be found perhaps in the Pauline letters. Whether we read his earlier letters or his later letters, invariably we see Paul trying to discern the pastoral situation of the communities in the light of the reign of God. Although Paul's thought about when God would realize his final plan seems to have evolved, what did not change was Paul's insistence on the crucial importance of that fulfillment. Paul's ethical teachings, his theological evaluation of sacramental praxis, and his exhortations to gospel-living are all grounded in his keen awareness of God's future: "After that will come the end, when, after having destroyed every sovereignty, authority, and power, he will hand over the kingdom to God the Father" (1 Cor. 15:24).

Those of us who are involved in the ministry of pastoral care can learn from Paul how to use God's kingdom as a measure of our own praxis. Obviously this eschatological criterion does not provide solutions or rules for all the daily concerns of pastoral care, but it does provide a general frame of reference. Much of pastoral care deals with the psychological pain, the physical suffering, or the social injustice experienced by individuals. If pastoral care is to deal adequately not only with the individual's need for healing but also with the larger social and cosmic evil that perpetuates such suffering, then God's larger vision must be our guide. Otherwise, faced with the mindless evil of torture or famine in a particular society, or of the suffering of an individual cancer patient or the family of an alcoholic, we may try to impart a comfort that does not look beyond the present.

A pastoral care praxis that does not assist individuals and communities to have a wider vision than that of their own private salvation may only encourage the confusion between apocalyptic and eschatological thought. Apocalyptic attitudes concentrate on the end-time in such a way that no sense of mission or responsibility is called forth. Eschatological vision brings us back to the present with a new sense of responsibility, and seriously challenges any privatized notion of a heaven earned by good conduct.

Where else are Christians to learn about the true nature of the kingdom to which they purportedly aspire, if not through the pastoral care that they receive throughout their life? Terminally sick Christians, for example, need a healing that prepares them for death and resurrection by the way in which they learn to accept the time remaining to them as both gift and call to service. The dying Christian, in this final praxis situation, can teach others about God's "new creation" better than any theological tract. The question is whether our pastoral care will call forth from the dying Christian this final gift of self.

There has always been a temptation to false eschatology. We usually ascribe Christians' misshapen ideas about the kingdom to poor religious education or preaching. But one suspects that the ultimate source of such false theology is the praxis of people's lives in which the needed private comfort given by pastoral care has not always been linked with a call to new service for the sake of God's kingdom.

Throughout this book we have referred repeatedly to the implicit definitions and models of grace, salvation, and church that are operative in our pastoral praxis. Doubtful models of the kingdom of God usually foster equally doubtful models of the church. Pastoral care praxis always reflects and helps to shape the implicit models of church that are operative in Christian experience. An example might be useful at this point.

### The Case of St. Joseph's Parish

St. Joseph's is a large middle- to upper-middle-class suburban parish. It has the financial strength to engage a religious education director, a choirmaster, and a youth minister. Two priests and two sisters function well as a pastoral team. From a ritual point of view the Sunday liturgies are generally celebrated well and attended well. The preaching, at its best, is thoughtful in content and relevant in style. In other words, this is a parish that by many standards would probably be considered above average. Most parishioners of St. Joseph's like their parish.

If it were possible to do a computer profile of the pastoral care being done at St. Joseph's, however, we might be surprised by the actualities of the pastoral situation. As a result of the two or three hundred hours of pastoral care being expended each week by all concerned, what are the results in terms of gospel-living and commitment? Such a question, of course, admits of no reliable answer. But anyone engaged in pastoral care routinely encounters many of the implicit models of church that result from what parishioners perceive their parish and its ministries to be about. The profile of pastoral care at St. Joseph's would reflect, first of all, these implicit models of the church.

### Sources of the Implicit Models

If in the minds of the Christians at St. Joseph's the function of the church, for example, is to be a spiritual "filling station," where individual needs for the sacraments, religious education, and counseling are met, then this deficient ecclesial model must be challenged and modified—for the effect of such a model is to limit the vision and service of good people. The model itself may result from the pastoral care actually being given by the ministry team, which in terms of style, structure, theological formation, and ritual celebration is that of St. Joseph's: thoroughly post–Vatican II. In addition to this spiritual "filling station" approach, there may well be a whole spectrum of ecclesial models represented in the praxis and theory of the parishioners and ministers of the parish. The limited purpose of this example is to illustrate how pastoral care actually helps to shape these implicit ecclesial models.

*Ministers*

Pastoral ministers are undoubtedly the first and primary source of such models. For better or worse, parishioners unreflectively perceive and absorb the attitudes of the team ministry in its praxis. Bureaucratic, needs-oriented, or person-oriented attitudes are easily recognized, whatever the theological background of the pastoral care person. Often enough this subtle dimension of ministry is scarcely noted. The team at St. Joseph's may have been trained in a post–Vatican II theology which they preach and teach to others. But parishioners read the team's operative understandings of church by the numerous ways in which the team's ministry toward them is expressed.

If, for example, the preaching at St. Joseph's never touches on the larger issues of social justice, nuclear armaments, or peace, then an implicit but nonetheless definite image of church is thereby imparted, one in which these issues are either marginal to or totally divorced from the sacramental and moral life of the community. In effect, this lack represents a negative praxis that has behind it a deficient theory of the church. If the team ministry is to accomplish its full ministry, then these missing aspects of the church must also be included in the preaching and in all other activities of the community.

Mette has put his finger on the problem implicit in such a pastoral situation when he reminds us that the wide-ranging concerns of pastoral care include both institutional and individual dimensions, both social and political arenas, and both ethical and liturgical concerns. All too often we tend to equate the institutional activity of the church with its Christian activity.[16] To do so is a mistake. In South America, for instance, a local church may be less than prophetic when it comes to confronting torture or poverty; such a failure of praxis is not to be confused with the true Christian praxis to which God's Word calls us. In other words, the concrete praxis of the first-century Corinthian church—or any church today—is not to be mistaken for what Paul says the church should be doing. There is such a thing as a negative praxis.

A sound theology of pastoral care reminds those engaged in caring ministry to critically reexamine the model of "church" out of which they are currently operating. How does their sense of church motivate them to carry on their particular ministries? How do they see their care affecting the mission of the local church? Do their priorities in pastoral care actually parallel and express their understanding of the church's mission?

### Individuals

A second source of our implicit models of the church is the praxis of individuals in the community. The presence of committed Christians has always been a constant source of good theology about the church. Dorothy Day or Mother Teresa might be accounted in some respects to have a conservative theology of the church and yet their radical personal commitment to the gospel brings us back to key Pauline teachings about the church in a way that no monograph on ecclesiology could do.

### Groups

In a similar way the Cursillo and Marriage Encounter groups in a parish usually represent a potential source for enriching other dimensions of the church. Their presence in the parish community can quietly challenge the privatized notions of church even as it invites parishioners to a reconsideration of how much of a role the church plays and should play in their own continuing conversion.

## Prophetic Renewal

An important task of pastoral care, after all, is to evoke prophetic witness from individuals in the Christian community. By "prophetic" I do not mean the dramatic and sometimes heroic activities of an Old Testament Isaiah or a New Testament Agabus, but rather the more humble though equally important tasks of clarifying, building, and bonding that characterize all prophecy. Such tasks are examples of the practical ways in which the Christian community is constantly renewed and our working models of church reevaluated and revised.

Once again the catechumenal process is instructive. In suggesting ways in which the catechumen matures, the *Rite of Christian Initiation of Adults* mentions a "transition, which brings with it a progressive change of outlook and morals that should become evident together with its social consequences and should be gradually developed during the time of the catechumenate."[17] The Christian community in general and the catechumenal team in particular share this responsibility of assisting catechumens to accept their own tasks for the sake of the kingdom of God. With such a change of outlook, the catechumen learns a praxis of church that entails not simply receiving care but also caring pastorally for the world.

But I understand "catechumen" to mean not only those seeking to be initiated into the Christian community, but also the already baptized who have begun to appropriate the meaning and cost of rituals celebrated some time ago. Each parish community is filled with people who have not yet realized, or are only beginning to realize, the implications of being Christian. Pastoral care has a privileged role in helping such people understand that a new outlook on the purpose of our lives and gifts makes the difference between being either a renewed disciple of Christ or a passive member of an institution.

Earlier in this chapter we cited the need for the local church to clarify and specify how God's kingdom and its values are being expressed in its pastoral care. The kingdom can be hampered or blocked by the specific forms of radical sin to which we have grown accustomed in our particular culture—blatant consumerism, racism, insensitive treatment of the elderly and the poor. Social attitudes and customs sometimes appear so sanitized and respectable that we no longer see the radical sin they embody and disguise. A failure to deal with these concrete examples of sin in our midst prevents the church from knowing the tasks and mission to which it must call its people. The local church, for example, can as a matter of priority in pastoral care emphasize sacramental preparation—a laudable concern in itself. But the honesty and commitment that each sacrament requires is clarified by the practical ways in which the local Christian community also calls us to witness against radical sin and to take up specific forms of service that help to deal with sinful situations.

## THE CRUCIAL IMPORTANCE OF PRAXIS

A major danger in pastoral care is that in doing our day-to-day work we may lose sight of our long-range purpose. The history of pastoral care is filled with examples of the dichotomy between theory and praxis. Throughout this book a plea has been made for observing more closely and analyzing more carefully our concrete pastoral praxis and its theological implications. Such analysis can result in both a deepening of theological insight and a more authentically pastoral praxis.

Whatever the form of pastoral care, Christian people are being formed by it—for better or for worse—in their understanding and praxis of the gospel message. There is little value in teaching the theological insights that Vatican II retrieved for our time if in its praxis the pastoral care of the local church is unwittingly teaching a less-complete doctrine. In particular, the Christian community's awareness of what salvation, church, and kingdom must mean for them will be influenced by the pastoral care which they experience and in which they participate. A crucial test for pastoral care is the perceptive and prophetic ways in which it invites participation in the message of the gospel by sharing the work of that gospel.

CHAPTER 5

# Theological Issues
# in
# Pastoral Care

On the eve of his death in 1949 Cardinal Suhard, a great pioneer in new forms of pastoral care, issued a pastoral letter to the priests of Paris which was destined to have an influence far beyond the confines of his diocese. In his *Priests Among Men* he argued for a rethinking of pastoral theology and for breaking away from methods suited to medieval Christianity.[1] This effort is to be based on a praxis guideline for which Suhard gave the following formulation: "to live in such a way that one's life would not make sense if God did not exist. To be a witness is much less a matter of external changes in one's way of living than of firm determination to establish a real community of destiny with the disinherited masses."[2]

Historically such guidelines, in one form or another, have always been a part of the perennial wisdom of pastoral caring for others. Martin of Tours in the fifth century and Francis of Assisi in the thirteenth century were familiar with such guidelines; they implemented them with pastoral creativity and success. The application of such norms is now the task before us.

Vatican II recognized—as had Trent—the need to assess and revitalize the church's mission to the world. Early in the "Dogmatic Constitution on the Church" (*Lumen Gentium*), the council proclaimed its belief that God "continually distributes in His Body, that is, in the Church, gifts of ministries through which, by His own power, we serve each other unto salvation so that, carrying out the truth in love, we may through all things grow up into Him who is our head."[3]

But in each era such general theological statements need concretely to be applied. In "The Church Today" (*Gaudium et Spes*) the council recognized the "duty of scrutinizing the signs of the times and of interpreting them in the light of the gospel."[4] Vatican II saw this effort as applied faith which would both enlighten our shared vocation in this world and help us arrive at solutions "which are fully human."[5] In evangelizing, the local church would have to adapt to various cultures and situations, with the help of people "versed in different institutions and specialties," for this is the task of all the people of God.[6]

Behind the objective and dispassionate statements of Vatican II, however, was a period of forty years of expanding pastoral care. Monsignor Joseph Cardijn, for example, had successfully begun the Young Christian Workers movement in Belgium. At the heart of Cardijn's movement was the conviction that young Christians themselves were in the best position to care pastorally for their alienated peer group. The priest-worker movement in France, which reached its peak in the forties, and the domestic Mission de France were attempts to reshape ministry according to the pastoral needs of the postwar era. The Grail movement and the Young Christian Workers movement in English-speaking countries were a creative catalyst for a whole generation of people seeking to bring the gospel message into the market place. Yves Congar's theological writings on the role of the laity, in particular, gave an inspiring basis for much of this work.[7]

The purpose of this chapter is not to add some practical corollaries to the theology of pastoral care thus far proposed, but to examine some of the specific theological issues which underlie the work of pastoral care. Three areas of concern have been singled out: the education needed for pastoral care ministries, the team ministry model of pastoral care, and some theological challenges to the priorities of pastoral care.

## EDUCATING FOR PASTORAL CARE

In its decree on priestly formation Vatican II forcefully insisted on the "pastoral concern which should thoroughly penetrate the entire training of seminarians."[8] The council then went on to spell out the aim of such pastoral concern, namely, to lead people "to a Christian life which is fully conscious and apostolic."[9] Seminarians will show that they have learned "this act of exercising the apostolate not only in theory but also in practice" by their ability to dialogue, to listen, and to respond.[10] These pastoral aims are applicable to both ordained and nonordained ministers of pastoral care.

### Historical Review

If we were to review the history of the American priesthood and its educational models, what would emerge would be its unique, immigrant, frontier, and missionary characteristics and its search for a better response to the pastoral needs of each era. But this is only one dimension of the American history of pastoral care in the Roman Catholic church. The care of the poor and the sick and the education of Catholics and non-Catholics were also undertaken by members of religious communities and lay people who sometimes provided prophetic challenge to the work of the clergy.

My purpose here is not to give a historial assessment of the success of this pastoral care, but to point out how the praxis of these four hundred years was generally more creative than the theory of the times. When a network of seminaries began to be established in the United States in the nineteenth century, they generally followed the classical theological formation of European seminaries.[11] The dimensions of pastoral care were, often enough, reduced to the solution of moral questions from casuistic cases and apologetics.

When Cardinal Gibbons wrote *The Ambassadors of Christ* in 1896 America was in many areas still a missionary country. In this influential book which, like the work of Frederick Schulze and William Stang,[12] was to serve as a text in the formation and education of seminarians and as an inspirational text for priests, Gibbons outlines his pastoral concerns in a way reminiscent of Gregory the Great's *Pastoral Care.*[13]

Gibbons discusses the virtues, attitudes, and learning necessary in one who cares for others. To his credit Gibbons firmly situates the classical teaching on priesthood within the American political and social scene at the end of the nineteenth century. When he turns to the pastoral care of people, the cardinal pinpoints what for him are the pastoral priorities: preaching, catechetical work, home and Sunday school, parochial schools, instruction of converts, congregational singing, and sick calls. Dedication, learning, kindness, and a sense of the times are seen as essential pastoral characteristics. In essence, Cardinal Gibbons aptly summarizes the perennial pastoral wisdom of his time within the context of the American situation. In doing so he also documents the strengths and weaknesses of pastoral care education in his time—and during the opening decades of the twentieth century.

While professional models, such as the lawyer's rhetorical abilities or the doctor's selfless care for the sick, are proposed by Gibbons to motivate the priest in his pastoral ministry, the underlying sense of church as community and of mission has all the limitations one might expect of nineteenth-century theology. The initial experiments in pastoral care education in the German universities of that time, briefly alluded to above in our discussion of the triumph of functionalism in chapter 4, seem to have made little impact in Catholic seminaries of the United States. This was due, no doubt, to the influence of the French Sulpician model of seminary training which emphasized personal spirituality coupled with classical theological formation of the student.

## The Current Situation

After World War II the Roman Catholic understanding of pastoral care began to expand. The work of such French priest-psychologists as Raymond Hostie[14] and André Godet[15] as well as that of John R. Cavanagh and Charles A. Curran in the United States, for example, made American priests aware of the need for a certain professionalism and for counseling skills.[16] These influences also appeared in much-read books of the sixties by George Hagmaier and Robert Gleason, Josef Goldbrunner, and C. W. Brister.[17] In the seventies the popular work of Henri Nouwen, reflecting both the theological concern of Vatican II and the pastoral psychology of Seward Hiltner, had a wide audience.[18] These psychological contributions to pastoral care provoked a great deal of discussion in recent decades about the danger of psychologism in pastoral care, and about the distinction between the role of the therapist and that of the confessor.

It is interesting to compare this body of rather sophisticated literature in pastoral care—which makes both explicit and implicit demands for psychological congruence and for more extensive professional training of its practitioners—with the psychological investigations published in *The Catholic Priest in the United States*.[19] The latter, an extensive study commissioned by the Catholic hierarchy of the United States in 1967, presents some challenging questions to those engaged in both ordained and nonordained ministries of pastoral care. While it is true that some of these problems are perhaps endemic to the celibate clergy, and hence not applicable to the growing body of lay ministers in the church, other questions suggested by the study cannot so easily be put aside.

The problem of intellectualization, for example, is certainly not limited to priests. Intellectualization might be described as a defense mechanism in which complex and challenging experience is reduced to a one-dimensional, rational solution. This defense allows a person to avoid the differences between the ideal self and the real self.

Another problem in personal growth indicated by the study is that of integrated psychosexual identity. In the experience of some priests the sexual dimension, instead of being a source of insight and responsible intimacy, is a confusing and misconstrued area that usually is externally controlled but internally unclarified.[20]

Perhaps the most important finding in the study is the general inability on the part of undeveloped priests to "articulate a deep level of personal religious faith." This problem accurately mirrors the unreflected and shallow experience of priests who substitute religious formulations for the task of dealing with religious meaning in their life.[21] The result is an unappropriated faith that is difficult to proclaim to others except in the form of theoretical statements.

These findings are a challenge to any system that claims to educate not only priests but all ministers of pastoral care. In varying degrees hospital ministry, religious education, youth ministry, and parish ministry of course require specific professional training. But the ultimate concern and goal of any such training must be ministers who are themselves credible if flawed models of what they proclaim in their work—models of that healing and justifying love of God that enables us too to serve and heal.

There is still too much pastoral care education that only reenforces in ministers of the gospel their sterile intellectualization, dysfunctional sexuality, and unappropriated faith. Theologically speaking such preparation for the ministries of the church deals only with God's action (*ex opere operato*), without enabling us to clarify our response (*ex opere operantis*). Unlike a Paul of Tarsus or Augustine of Hippo, who learned to see the praxis of God in their own experience and thus to minister to others, a one-sided intellectual and professional training can blur our own needs and those of others.

Thanks to the influence of the Clinical Pastoral Education model (CPE), which combines a supervised pastoral experience with theological reflection on a specific critical personal experience, pastoral training in Roman Catholic seminaries and theological faculties has become more sensitive to such issues. Case study methods have also provided a complementary approach in which specific pastoral issues can be examined in concrete historical contexts. More recently James D. and Evelyn E. Whitehead have proposed another method of theological reflection, based on the thought of Bernard Lonergan and David Tracy, that questions the pastoral care minister on both the experiential and theological implications of a pastoral situation.[22] In the familiar threefold process of attending, asserting, and deciding, the minister is prompted to incorporate theological traditions, cultural information, and personal experience in such a way that truly ministerial action is facilitated.

## A Catechumenal Process

These approaches, with their emphasis on the larger social and cultural contexts, the tradition of the church, and the shared experience of the carers and those for whom they care, represent an important advance in pastoral education, as do the expanded pastoral care curricula and supervision in seminaries and theological schools. But in many theological and pastoral care departments there is still a great deal of teaching that speaks of experience but does not actually invite the participants to deal with it. As indicated in our discussion of the ecclesial context of ministry toward the close of chapter 3, it is a temptation for us professionals to question others about the very realities we are unwilling to face in our own lives. In theological education this temptation translates into a competent theoretical preparation—with the necessary number of pastoral care courses and supervised ministries along with their required verbatims and group work—but no deepened willingness to work through the question that such education should evoke.

When Mette, then, proposes a definition of pastoral activity as communicative activity in which distorted communications are replaced by a community of shared and appropriated meanings, he is suggesting an important theory about pastoral praxis.[23] Communicative activity, however, demands not only a consciousness but also an openness to all knowledge and experience, as Karl Rahner reminds us.[24] Authentic education for ministry must constantly invite the student to learn the meaning of the axiom: "Doctor, heal yourself."

One major component of any formation to pastoral care ministry, then, should be a replication of the catechumenal process with its call to see what God has done for us—in other words, spiritual autobiography. It is interesting to note, for example, how many religious people in the United States have found Ira Progoff's Intensive Journal techniques helpful for renewing their sense of self, their ability to symbolize their experience, and their sense of pastoral mission to others.[25] Yet this process is, in one sense, as old as Christianity itself. In retrieving our experience by discovering beyond the facts of our lives their meanings and challenges, we recognize our sin and our gifts, our need and God's grace. In turn, we learn compassion for those who have difficulty in confronting their own experience.

In one form or another, pastoral care must ultimately listen to and help clarify the story of the alcoholic, the cancer patient, the marginal and dispossessed, the young and the elderly. If these people cannot learn to pray and sacramentalize out of their own stories, what else can pastoral care do for them? Without such help, those to whom we minister will have no deeper capacity to symbolize their need in worship and sacrament. Without such help, are we not simply duplicating the social and health services that others sometimes do better than we?

## COMMUNAL CONTEXTS FOR PASTORAL CARE

Some of the problems—such as intellectualization, psychosexual identity, and the appropriation of faith—cited in the Catholic Bishops' study of the American priest[26] can become aggravated and remain unchallenged in an isolated living situation. Persons in nonordained ministries, whether they are living in religious communities or in families, may share these same problems, but a healthy and caring context can facilitate their ongoing conversion and can support their ministry.

For the theologian, however, this is not simply a question of psychological support groups. The very nature of New Testament discipleship centers on the shared and covenant nature of salvation and mission. There can be no separation between being the church and doing the work of the gospel.

### Koinōnia

*Koinōnia* is the word which best sums up this Pauline concern for being the church. The word has a wide range of meanings in Greek—from partnership to sharing, to being in communion. Whether *koinōnia* is expressed in the practical issue of a collection for poor Christians, or in giving the right hand of fellowship (Gal. 2:9) in recognition of a conclusive agreement at Jerusalem with the other apostles, for Paul the deeper ecclesial meaning was always present. J. Paul Sampley summarizes this theology in commenting on the meaning of *koinōnia* in the Letter to the Philippians: "The Philippians recognized their new situation in Christ and found themselves brought into a new association on a new basis. *Koinōnia* rang in their ears, not just of a fellowship of the faithful but as a partnership of the faithful. . . . They joined with Paul as equal partners in living and preaching the gospel."[27]

Paul's *phronein* ("being of the same mind," as in Phil. 2:2, 5) complements and explains *koinōnia*. Because of their relationship with one another in Christ, Christians have a communality of attitude and mission that prompts them to be of service and to share the work of pastoral care.[28] On this understanding, community and pastoral care are not two juxtaposed areas of Christian living but rather two aspects of the same reality. Paul's concept of an apostolic community that does the pastoral care demanded by gospel commitment is not to be confused with living in the same house, or being associated in the same type of work. Pauline participation or partnership is found in a disciple group who, by the way they live the gospel together, enable each other to minister, and by the way they minister to shape a credible community.

These Pauline insights were realized in the early Christian house-churches. The word "church" in current English usage connotes for most people an institutional group or a set of buildings, but this is not the Pauline understanding of the word. In his continuation of the familial language that Jesus employed ("brother/sister," for example, in Mark 3:34–35) and in his description of the community in terms of the body, Paul sketched out practical guidelines for the life of the church communities of his times. When Paul speaks of those who meet in the home of Prisca and Aquila (1 Cor. 16:19 and Rom. 16:1ff) or of the household of Stephanas, he is referring to people who both pray and minister together.[29]

This ideal of core Christian communities from which the many dimensions of pastoral care emanated was never completely lost in the Christian tradition. Religious communities such as the earlier monastic and later mendicant communities mirrored this ideal. Even among diocesan priests this communal context for pastoral care can be seen, for example, in Augustine's concern that his priests live in community, or in the medieval communities of cathedral priests who bound themselves by a rule, or in the twentieth-century model of team ministry.

## Team Ministry

"Team ministry" is an ambiguous phrase. For some, it describes a functional model in which a group of ministers share their pastoral care concerns, strategies, and decision making, and work together to achieve common aims in their ministry to others. This understanding of team ministry obviously does not demand shared life or even shared prayer, though these may actually be included in some form. In many ways this type of team ministry is no different from the team approach that is characteristic of the American business world—shared planning and problem solving for the sake of producing more effective results.

A different model of team ministry originated in France in the forties, in such parish communities as that of St. Séverin in Paris. This approach to team ministry was clearly modeled on a core Christian community or house-church. The ministries of such a community stemmed from and were enabled by a gospel-life in which the members' sharing of prayer and of what God was doing in their lives complemented the practical ministerial decisions they were making.

The reasoning behind this latter style of team ministry is as old as the Pauline *koinōnia*. Christians had been invited into a catechumenal process in which they would make up what was lacking in the sufferings of Christ (Col. 1:24) and would be the presence of Christ in this world. The contemporary model of this shared Christian life was a group of diocesan priests who enabled one another to do the work of the gospel. As one who lived in such a team ministry for several years at St. Séverin in Paris, I can testify to the dynamic and transforming experience that such a community affords. Although I had lived in religious communities for years before I came to St. Séverin, and in such groups had found support for my ministry, I found operative at St. Séverin a unique catechumenal dynamic within a team-ministry community.

Like all successful religious communities, the priests of St. Séverin knew how to evoke commitment from one another on many levels of living. Their preaching and pastoral care rang true because they spoke out of an imperfect but credible experience of a core Christian community. Their own sense of ministry and care invited others to participate in the pastoral care ministries of the community. From the way in which the team ministry lived, people perceived pastoral care first of all as a way of life, and not simply as things to do for the parish. As a result, two decades before Vatican II St. Séverin could boast of shared ministries and of a constantly renewed community. In a real sense the whole community and its many ministries were always in a catechumenal process.

There is a lesson for pastoral care in such a model. The success of such team-ministry structures does not depend primarily on people living together in the same house or doing rituals together. Marriage Encounter or Cursillo in the eighties, as the Young Christian Workers movement of the thirties, rests on similar experiences in which Christians learn to build living communities of shared religious meaning and pastoral care. In Marriage Encounter and Cursillo people from whom formerly nothing had been expected now learn to care pastorally for others. They become the house-churches of the eighties that a Prisca and Aquila would have no trouble recognizing.

Even in a parish served by only one priest, there are many members who can build such core communities of pastoral care. In learning so to build and care, both the priest and the members begin to share the responsibility of caring for one another in much the same way as did earlier generations of Christians. This is one of the major challenges to contemporary pastoral care. In a postindustrial society, where so much that passes for community is merely a convenient social grouping of people, the Christian community has a prophetic witness to give. God's future community is imperfectly but clearly experienced wherever two or three are gathered together in his name, and in the power of that name doing his work.

## THE PRIORITIES OF
## PASTORAL CARE

In the final scene of Leonard Bernstein's *Mass* the celebrant, perceiving the fragmented commitments of the group around him, tears off his vestments and sings: "Things get broken so easily." Throughout the song there is a careful interplay between the images of Eucharist as community and the image of Eucharist as the presence of Christ. With Pauline insistence Bernstein suggests that if Eucharist is to be realized in our midst all pastoral care must deal with both the brokenness of individuals and the divisions of the Christian community.

Anyone who has worked in the ministries of pastoral care knows how easily things get broken. Indeed, the argument of this book has been that all pastoral care is ultimately tested in the present, by the deepening unity of shared meaning and mission in a group of Christians, and in the future by the final unity we call the kingdom of God.

### The Testing

Paul's logic is irresistible: "To each person the manifestation of the Spirit is given for the common good" (1 Cor. 12:7). Any pastoral care that is authentically evangelical has always known how to help Christians transcend their private needs, and once again *be* on account of others. Whether the particular pastoral care ministry takes place in a hospital, among the poor, in prison, among youth or the elderly, the gospel priorities of pastoral care should be clear.

These priorities are tested first of all in praxis, not in theory. No matter what systematic theology may be saying about the nature of salvation, or practical theology may regard as crucial to pastoral care, Christians learn the key meanings of the gospel from the praxis we call pastoral care. If in the Christian community there is a sacramental praxis that seems to require little commitment and even less service, then this distorted praxis will account for the jettisoning of even the most sophisticated of ecclesial or sacramental theories.

Pastoral care has always had two particularly important tasks. The first is to forge credible communities of Christians that can proclaim the gospel. The second is to call forth the many "manifestations of the Spirit" in the ministries that are needed.[30]

The first task implies a gospel morality that is readily distinguishable from a Stoic or humanist morality. The law of Christ, understood as an exigent and transforming love that prefigures the kingdom, has little to do with detached rules of morality that have lost that eschatological frame of reference. Gospel care enables Christians willingly to appropriate Christ's law of love so that they can witness to a risen Lord.

The second task is equally important: our ongoing conversion is tested by our willingness to do the work of the gospel. In other words, God's Spirit, which is the root of all conversion and pastoral care, is not given to us for the sake of an idle holiness, but to serve the world's need for redemption. Like Peter on Pentecost, Christians have received the Spirit so that they may be his witnesses (Acts 2:32). These summary remarks, however, need themselves to be tested against one of the major concerns of pastoral care today, namely, ministry to youth.

### Youth Ministry

Eighteen hundred years ago the church quite successfully evoked such pastoral care from many of the pagan youth in the Roman Empire. The Roman martyrology is filled with the names of young Roman soldiers who, as catechumens, learned to care for others and to witness to the gospel even unto death. We do not necessarily achieve the same pastoral results today simply by hiring a youth minister.

The early church seems instinctively to have understood that the commitment demands of the gospel are a powerful invitation to invest oneself in the Christian community and its tasks. In contrast, many Christian communities today seem to have lost a sense of mission, and consequently to have difficulty evoking commitment from their young. Gospel commitment, after all, is tested by more than institutional attendance, financial support, and religious education.

When we analyze some of the more successful commitment models in American society today, we inevitably find a community that invites its members to a vision that is spelled out in terms of practical norms and tasks. The Peace Corps, Vista, the Moonies, the Mormons, and the Taizé youth movement represent widely disparate visions; yet they share a common success in being able to evoke commitment from youth. As Rosabeth Moss Kanter has convincingly argued, such successful communities offer within the framework of their communal/ecclesial purpose and tasks an identity and a sense of direction to young people.[31]

Much like the commitment demands that Hippolytus's third-century Christian community made on prospective catechumens in the *Apostolic Tradition,* these contemporary communities have redefined their vision in terms of the twentieth-century scene. As a result, personal and communal meanings are welded together.[32] If Christian communities will not look around their world more closely and question the social injustice, the ethics of the business world, and political and interpersonal issues with their corollaries of meaning, how can they hope to challenge the generosity and commitment of today's youth?

Youth ministry can only implement the vision of the larger Christian community. One suspects that such youth ministry has only the limited and short-term goals of getting the young to come to church or to participate in a "Search" weekend, without any viable follow-up that is based on a wider gospel vision. Once again effective pastoral care would involve inviting the young to discover how the deeper meanings of their own life are intertwined with those of the gospel.

Tomorrow's pastoral care ministers are growing up now in our midst. The Christian youth of today—for better or worse—are already learning their theologies from our praxis models of care. Many generous young people have either rejected active participation in the church as they know it, or are involved in fundamentalist groups. An important test of our pastoral care will be the response to service and mission of those who follow us.

In the final analysis, all pastoral care is active training in that mystery of God which we call salvation. No theology, systematic or practical, will ever begin to exhaust its riches. There is a danger that those who work in pastoral care might forget where their own efforts end and God's unearned mystery continues. Once again Paul provides an insight to match his own service in gospel care: "I became a minister of this church through the commission God gave me to preach among you his word in its fullness, that mystery hidden from ages and generations past but now revealed to his holy ones. . . . the mystery of Christ in you, your hope of glory. . . . For this I work and struggle, impelled by that energy of his which is so powerful a force within me" (Col. 1:25–27, 29).

CHAPTER 6

# Pastoral Care
# for
# Tomorrow

Praying before a crucifix in a small chapel outside his home-town, Francis of Assisi heard the challenge: "Rebuild my house." At first he understood the words in their literal sense and began to re-construct the dilapidated structure. Eventually the phrase came to have a more profound meaning for his entire life as he took it to mean that the gospel-life of the church was to be renewed. Fran-cis's effort to respond to that challenge proved to be the turning point of his life.

Throughout this book I have suggested that pastoral care cannot achieve its real purpose if it does not renew a sense of mission in all whom it touches. Pastoral care allows Christians to hear once more Christ's challenge: "Rebuild my house." It enables us who do not see or hear perfectly ourselves to help others see and hear again. Today the need for effective pastoral care is greater than ever because many Christians no longer perceive that challenge to help as an essential dimension of becoming or remaining authentically Chris-tian. Pastoral care retools Christians so that they can participate in this rebuilding with a new sense of purpose and vision. Our concern here is with pastoral care for tomorrow.

The purpose of this chapter is a modest one—to illustrate briefly the particular theology of pastoral care that has been espoused throughout this book. From the many areas routinely dealt with in pastoral care I have selected three that encompass a large segment of the people we attempt to care for pastorally—the sick, youth, and the elderly. Within each of these groups are obviously several sub-groups. Before dealing with these specific areas of pastoral concern, however, we must return to the model of pastoral care that was first introduced in the opening chapter.

## CATECHUMENAL GUIDELINES FOR
## PASTORAL CARE

Throughout this book we have alluded to the catechumenal process and to the importance of the catechumenate in uncovering our operative definitions of such central realities as salvation, church, sin, and mission. Catechumens, it was noted, learn praxis definitions of salvation by the way in which the Word of God urges them to be of service and to cast a fresh eye on the need of others. To enter upon such service is to follow the Pauline injunction, "As Christ, so we." Sin is perceived, in particular, as a life lived without commitment to gospel values. The church, in praxis, is experienced in its lived priorities of witness, mission, and worship. The ministries within such a church evolve from a keen sense of shared mission.

But have such a church and such catechumens ever existed? Yes, in every epoch there have always been imperfect but authentic Christian communities and candidates because in every age there has always been flawed but effective pastoral care. If initiation is indeed the model of all that the church does and celebrates, then the way in which candidates prepare for initiation should serve as a model for pastoral care. Certainly the catechumenate in its four stages can provide guidelines for pastoral care.

### Evangelization

A crucial element in the precatechumenal stage is evangelization. Whether we look again at the young Roman soldier in the second century or at the Christian today who is considering a return to the practice of his or her faith, the Word of God is the key. But this Word is always proclaimed in order that God may make all things new again among us. In the words of the *Rite of Christian Initiation of Adults,* evangelization should touch all members of the community so that "together with the catechumens, the faithful reflect upon the value of the paschal mystery, renew their own conversion, and by their example lead the catechumens to obey the Holy Spirit more generously."[1] This summary of the effects of the catechumenal process on the Christian community is equally accurate as a description of the results of effective pastoral care. Indeed the catechumenal process actually suggests to those who work in pastoral care what could be regarded as a first guideline: *Effective pastoral care leads to ongoing conversion and renewal.*

But such ongoing conversion and renewal is prompted by the process of inquiry that evangelization always sets in motion. As suggested earlier, the Word of God always unsettles our self-serving interpretations of the gospel by asking the penetrating questions we would rather not deal with. Further, evangelization is not only the source of such questions; God's Word actually trains us repeatedly to revise the questions in appropriate ways as we go about living our own life.

Pastoral care has as one of its tasks the retooling of Christians so that they may learn again both to hear the insistent gospel questions and to pose such questions to themselves and to others. Radical sin, in one of its more anodyne forms, expresses itself in the complacency afforded by comfortable answers, when we feel no need for the new and searching questions God's Word suggests. Sick persons, for example, may believe that the answer to their situation is "the will of God"—without questioning what new witness may be demanded by their condition. The chemically dependent person may think that the Christian solution to such a problem is control—without asking what new service is called for as a result of the struggle. Average Christians may feel that they are already sensitive to the needs of the poor—and never question whether their charity needs to take on new forms and greater breadth.

In contrast to a pastoral care which does nothing but comfort and assuage, the evangelization of the precatechumenal period offers a mode of inquiry in which God's Word questions both the purposes of pastoral care and the current vision of the people for whom we care. In the sacramental dimension of pastoral care, for example, is the Word of God seen merely as a ritual requirement, or is it regarded rather as a necessary help toward honest participation in Christ's mission? In determining the priorities of pastoral care in a parish or hospital ministry, does the Word of God call in question the moments and the ways in which we minister? Does the Word of God continue to call forth new ministries of care from established Christian communities?

To return to our hypothetical example in chapter 4, St. Joseph's would probably be rated an above-average parish in its pastoral care and in its liturgical celebrations. The danger with such a relevant community, however, as we noted earlier, is that it may come to be regarded as a spiritual "filling station" for Christians. Suppose that a proposal is made to open a soup kitchen or a halfway house for drug-addicted people within the parish boundaries of St. Joseph's. Opposition is voiced by a segment of the parish who would be happy perhaps to contribute financially to such a cause, but do not want to locate within their parish borders the potential problems that such a ministry might entail. How can the pastoral care of St. Joseph's team ministry deal with the implicit and hidden yet precise and inadequate definitions of church and salvation that are operative in this situation?

At the heart of the more-successful diocesan and parish renewal programs presently in use in the United States, evangelization as sharing of the Word of God plays a central role. People begin to take responsibility for God's Word and to inquire again about the practical corollaries of the gospel in their own situation. The opposition of some parishioners to a soup kitchen or a halfway house within St. Joseph's parish may betray a lack of evangelical responsibility and inquiry. This pastoral situation, in turn, may reflect a missing dimension in the pastoral care of the team ministry at St. Joseph's.

While the theology of the Word of God again enjoys a privileged position in post–Vatican II theological reflection, pastoral praxis and liturgical ritual have not always for the average Christian translated this theology into a living concern. An evangelization that leads to honest questioning and more authentic prayer can be implemented in many ways. But the most common and accessible form of evangelization continues to be the small group of Christians who "break the bread" of God's Word by reflecting on it together and praying out of such reflection.

## Catechumenal Intentions

The expected result of evangelization—within the catechumenal process—is that persons may make "their intention known to the Church."[2] A candidate for initiation is someone who has already experienced an "initial conversion and desire to change one's life and to enter into contact with God in Christ, thus the first sense of repentance and the practice of calling on God and praying; and the first experience of the society and spirit of Christians."[3] Yet many Christians do not seem to have arrived at the commitments expected of a candidate for initiation. For them, beyond the first meaning and experience of repentance and conversion, the catechumenal process suggests what could thus be regarded as a second guideline for those who work in pastoral care: *Effective pastoral care enables those already initiated to clarify their intentions.*

People who minister to others can learn pastoral realism from the catechumenal process. Even though the candidate already evidences a certain Christian experience and witness, the person's intentions are crucial if there is to be growth. Our intentions cut through the activities and theories of our living; they examine our values and motivations, our operative definitions and visions of the future. There is no easier way for Christians to deceive themselves than to assume that their unexamined intentions are honest and evangelical.

If our pastoral care does not in some way lead Christians back to their intentions, of what use is all the rest? Youth ministry at St. Joseph's, for example, is a priority of the pastoral care team. But, as any youth minister can testify, a great deal of time can be expended on youth activities without ever getting to a process within which these young people, both communally and individually, can reexamine the driving forces of their lives. In contrast, the Young Christian Workers movement was built on a process in which young people began to uncover their own and their society's operative intentions. This led to a decision-making process in which participants committed themselves to apostolic activity.

The catechumenal process seems to include a similar emphasis. The *Rite of Christian Initiation of Adults* cites apostolic activity as one of four major ways for helping candidates mature: "Since the Church's life is apostolic, catechumens should also learn how to work actively with others to spread the Gospel and build up the Church by the testimony of their lives and the profession of their faith."[4] An important element in the life of all Christians is the intention to witness to the gospel in a way that is appropriate to their situation, gifts, and life-stage. For many Christians the resultant activity may appear ordinary if not banal, but the key factor is the underlying intention.

Another pastoral example is that of marriage. A major pastoral care concern today is the high percentage of marriages that end in divorce. Current canonical practice is increasingly sensitive in recognizing the various causes for annulment of marriage among the baptized. But this does not answer the underlying question: Do the intentions of this couple reach beyond the bonds of a civil marriage contract to include the specific elements of a sacrament?

At St. Joseph's, preparation for marriage is taken seriously. Teams composed of pastoral staff and committed Christian couples dialogue with prospective couples in preparation for the celebration of their marriage within the church community. But an adequate theology of pastoral care should help these teams to sensitize young couples to their own motivation in wishing to be married in the church and help them to appropriate the larger values of such a marriage. Obviously, a couple's intentions about the sacrament of marriage can extend no further than their intentions about the sacrament of initiation. If they have not yet intended what the church intends—to be "as Christ"—then it will be difficult for them to embrace and act on a sacramental view of marriage.

The pastoral care of such a couple must accordingly be more than simply informational or inspirational. The marriage preparation teams at St. Joseph's have as one of their principal tasks the clarification and broadening of the young couple's intentions in asking to be married within the Christian community. In addition to questions about the quality of their relationship and their desire for a family, the marriage preparation team has a task similar to that of a catechumenal team. Like catechumens, this couple needs the help of other committed Christians so that they can stretch their attitudes about the role of their love in building up the body of Christ, the Christian community. The question addressed to sponsors and to the Christian assembly concerning prospective catechumens might appropriately be addressed to the marriage preparation team at St. Joseph's about this couple: "You have heard them declare their resolve. Do you testify that they have chosen Christ as Lord and that they wish to serve him alone?"[5]

## Enlightened Sacraments

Within the Roman Catholic tradition sacramental ministry has always been an important part of pastoral care. We have already pointed to some of the dangers inherent in such an emphasis: privatized notions of sacrament, a lack of ecclesial and eschatological perspective in the sacramental participation, and a search for comfort without deeper commitment to the gospel and its work. Since Vatican II the role of the sacraments in pastoral care has received new attention. One traditional resource for such a fresh discussion is the catechumenal process in which Christians originally learned the meaning of the sacraments for their lives. Pastoral care can still learn much about sacramental ministry from this same source.

The period immediately preceding the sacraments of initiation (baptism, confirmation, Eucharist) is accurately called "purification and enlightenment or illumination."[6] It is the period of Lent during which persons are prepared for the feast of the paschal mystery, Easter. It was in this special context that the sacraments of initiation were received by the elected catechumens.[7] Unlike most Catholics today, who have received these sacraments as infants and young children, adult catechumens in earlier times were prepared to enter into this unified sacramental experience from a different context. During the first scrutiny on the Third Sunday of Lent the celebrant says to the community about those elected to be initiated at Easter:

"The Church has confidently chosen these men and women whose long preparation will be over at Easter. Let us pray that they will be ready and will find Christ in his sacraments."[8]

In a very real sense the ancient axiom that "the law of worship is the law of belief" (*lex orandi lex credendi*) is best illustrated in this reception of the Easter sacraments by those who have spent years as catechumens. These Easter sacraments of initiation summarize the catechumens' spiritual journey of conversion, symbolize God's gratuitous offer to them of an unearned salvation in Christ, and elicit their commitment to the work of the gospel. All of the other rites, such as the baptismal questioning, the anointing of the catechumens with oil, the bestowal of the white garment and lighted candle, are filled with the language of commitment. In brief, participation in the sacraments of initiation (the law of worship) teaches very clearly the response that God enables each Christian to give (the law of belief).

In Christian praxis and teaching, sacraments have always been associated with pastoral care and healing. At the same time, pastoral experience has always had to deal with the difficulties of honest and realistic sacramental participation (in traditional theological language, *ex opere operantis*). The catechumenal process thus suggests yet another practical guideline to those who work in pastoral care: *Sacraments that heal always enable the healed persons to do the work of Christ.*

In teaching Christians the purpose of sacraments in their lives, pastoral ministers can derive some direction from this catechumenal guideline. Sacraments are a tangible dimension of Christians' day-to-day lives. As symbols of Christ's real presence in the church, sacraments can clarify the meaning and direction of our life and at each stage enable us to appropriate our initiation. Yet two decades after Vatican II the pastoral care dimension of sacramental ministry remains a complex problem.

What are the pastoral expectations of the church, for example, when divorced Catholics wish to receive the Eucharist? In demanding that Catholics attend mass on Sundays (and presumably participate fully by receiving the Eucharist), how do we invite these Christians to move past juridical obligation or privatized devotion to the Pauline "proclaiming the death of the Lord until . . ."? While we insist that young people receive Confirmation, do we on a pastoral level remain ambiguous about how this new sacramental responsibility should affect and change their participation in the local church?

Pastoral care has always played an important role, whether in shaping or in deforming sacramental praxis. Sacramental theology may propose penetrating insights, but pastoral care deals with the specific situations and with the particular communities as they try to participate more honestly in the sacraments. If the thesis is accepted that sacramental healing also involves ecclesial mission, then a complementary but difficult pastoral task is that of spelling out the sacramental implications in a particular church. The sacramental praxis of marriage, for example, would change considerably if the local church developed specific norms for how a couple may fulfill their symbolic role of witnessing to the love of Christ for the church.

Anointing of the sick provides yet another example. Healing in the Christian tradition is a fulfillment of the messianic promise and a witness to the continuing compassionate love of God for his people. But pastoral care has a creative role to play in the authentic celebration of this sacrament. Do we empower those who are healed by asking for this particular gift in order that they can undertake this particular ministry—for example, the ministry of visiting the sick—to the extent that this is at all a possibility?

In brief, if pastoral care in the Roman Catholic community today is to be faithful to its sacramental tradition, it must be as creative as its predecessors have been. Historically, the church has not hesitated in its celebration and praxis of sacraments to make significant changes because of the general pastoral principle, "sacraments are for the sake of the people" (*sacramentum propter hominem*). The change from canonical to Irish tax penance in the sixth and seventh centuries and the extension of the so-called Petrine privilege in annulment of marriages in the twentieth century are but two well-known examples of this pastoral principle. The pastoral care of our time is challenged to rethink its sacramental praxis with the help of this same principle.

## The Mondays of Faith

As in any relationship, initial enthusiasm for and commitment to the gospel is tested in the usually banal situations of our living out the faith. Often enough, catechumens seem to have been prepared for a church that does not even exist. The newly initiated move from a closely knit core community of Christians to the larger and more anonymous parish community. How do they find their place within such communities?

The *Rite of Christian Initiation of Adults* presents the theological theory of what should happen: "They have been renewed in mind, have tasted more intimately the good word of God, have shared in the Holy Spirit, and have come to discover the goodness of the Lord.

From this experience, which is proper to the Christian and is increased by the way he lives, they draw a new sense of the faith, the Church and the world."[9] This is in fact what the sacraments of initiation make possible—but there are a number of variables.

As any pastoral minister knows, large numbers of parishioners can be fairly content with minimal participation in the life of the local church. This reflects a praxis in opposition to the principle stated above. For many Christians the sacraments have nothing to do with the mission of the church. If average Catholics expect, or perhaps want, nothing more than a competent preaching of the Word, regular celebration of sacraments, and adequate religious education for their children, their praxis view of the church may differ sharply from that of the newly baptized adult who has spent a considerable time preparing to *be* church, and not simply to take up space in a church. This tension reflects the problem of the final state of adult initiation, the postbaptismal or mystagogical period.

Once again, because the initiation process is a model for the whole Christian life, we can learn from this catechumenal stage an important principle for a theology of pastoral care. This principle, in fact, is enunciated in the rite itself; the postbaptismal period is crucial because "neophytes, helped by their sponsors, may enter into a closer relationship with the faithful and bring them renewed vision and new impetus."[10] For pastoral care the principle might be restated in this way: *The quality of Christian community engendered by effective pastoral care is always tested by the wider vision and deepened commitment of all the baptized.*

In the catechumenal process, sponsors are ideally the representatives of the Christian community who accompany the candidates on their spiritual journey by the way in which they encourage, teach, give example to, and pray with them. In this final stage these sponsors are the bridge between the newly baptized and the larger Christian community; they help in the integration of the neophytes into the mission of the local church. In similar fashion the pastoral care minister assumes these same responsibilities of nurturing and of evoking the giving of themselves on the part of the young, the sick, the marginal, and the many others who need such care—so that they may once more enter into the active life of the church. Again, the catechumenal theme suggests the larger pastoral ramifications: "Great care should be taken that they obtain full and joyful insertion into the life of the community."[11]

For the sponsor and the catechumen "insertion into the life of the community" does not mean passive membership in a pious association. The Pauline teaching is a guide to understanding what integration or reintegration into the community should mean: "You, then, are the body of Christ. Every one of you is a member of it" (1 Cor. 12:27). Within the context of Paul's letter, this reminder is a call to responsible service. A pastoral care praxis that forgets this Pauline teaching is likely to operate with short-range objectives in which the parish's present self-definition and expectations actually blur the gospel challenge.

Pastoral care cannot hope to answer all the needs of the community if, as in the catechumenal process, it does not elicit the help of sponsors, people whose ministry has been evoked by the need of others.[12] Sponsors in pastoral care are those who walk the Christian way with others, assisting the very people from whom they also learn. Sponsors are a proof of the vitality of pastoral care in a community because they have responded to the gospel challenge not to be served but to give oneself for the sake of others (Mark 10:45). Some of the practical corollaries of sponsoring will be suggested in the following sections, all of which represent attempts to illustrate our proposed theology of pastoral care.

## THE SICK

In chapter 3 we presented a privileged symbol of pastoral care, that of the *medicus* or "doctor." We saw that the biblical notion of healing encompasses both the conversion that God makes possible and the forgiveness that he continues to give. Mark 2:17 in particular, with its reminder that the sick (sinners) need a doctor, inspired insightful patristic commentaries and a creative pastoral care praxis. The gradual transposition of this doctor image into a juridical one was also noted.

The *medicus* discussion also provided the occasion for briefly analyzing the professional model of ministry and the peculiar temptation of Roman Catholic theology, since the Donatist heresy, to minimize the subjective aspects of ministry in order to safeguard the objective and gratuitous nature of God's saving action. To retrieve the *medicus* symbol for our own era, we proposed the catechumenal process. The guidelines for the praxis of pastoral care which we have just drawn from the four periods of the catechumenate continued this line of thought from chapter 3.

### Meaning in Illness

As anyone in pastoral care well knows, the sick, like the poor, are always with us and absorb a good deal of pastoral time and effort. In recent years hospital ministries have benefited from the general professional specialization that has gone on in all aspects of health care. This has resulted in a higher level of psychosocial training and sensitivity on the part of pastoral ministers and more fruitful interaction with other health care personnel. In one sense this is a historical continuation of the role that the church assumed early on in the care of the sick, the erection of hospitals, and the foundation of religious communities devoted to the care of the physically and mentally ill.

The theological question that persists in all these historical developments is whether the comfort and care that is given is unintentionally privatized and limited. In other words, applying the four guidelines derived from the catechumenal process to the care of the sick: Does this ministry heal in the biblical sense? Does the care of the sick have an evangelization component that allows them to ask new questions about their lives and to clarify their intentions? Do the sacraments administered to the sick enable them to do the work of Christ in a way that is appropriate to their life-stage and situation? Does the pastoral care of these sick permit a wider vision and a deeper commitment to the gospel and its mission? The post–Vatican II rituals for the anointing and eucharizing of the sick provide a rich praxis theology that can help us answer such questions.[13]

Vatican II corrected a pastoral praxis in which the anointing of the sick had gradually become the sacrament of extreme unction, the sacrament of the dying.[14] This conciliar return to the earlier tradition of the church is stated eloquently in *Lumen Gentium*: "By the sacred anointing of the sick and the prayer of her priests, the whole Church commends those who are ill to the suffering and glorified Lord, asking that He may lighten their suffering and save them (cf. James 5:14–16). She exhorts them, moreover, to contribute to the welfare of the whole People of God by associating themselves freely with the passion and death of Christ."[15] The best way to comment theologically on the council's statement is to examine the ritual for the anointing of the sick, which fleshed out its pastoral implications.

In the introduction to the new rite for anointing and care of the sick, sickness is presented within the Christian understanding. From Jesus' care of the sick and from his teaching the church sees meaning and value in this suffering.[16] The messianic healing of Jesus would be misunderstood if it were reduced merely to a kind of validation of his claims. Sight to the blind and hearing to the deaf are messianic symbols that reveal humankind's need of redemption, and thus allow each one to welcome the sheer gift of God's abundance.[17]

Sickness, in other words, is a multivalent symbol that makes people vulnerable on many levels of their experience. In the language of Paul Ricoeur sickness is usually a limit-experience in which people find their plans and goals, their values and commitments suddenly called into question. The movement from health to sickness can also represent a change from unreflective living to serious questioning of one's motives and meanings.

Ricoeur's point is that limit-experiences such as sickness permit us to reappropriate religious language as limit-expression.[18] Once more the kingdom of God is taught in the parables of our experience, and we learn to cry out to God from the radical need that is just below the surface of our neat and ordered lives. Without such limit-experiences we might remain blind and deaf, thinking that we had sight and hearing. Sickness, then, is always a potential turning point in our Christian self-awareness and vision. Jesus' reply to his questioners about the cause of the young man's blindness is to the point: "It was to let God's works show forth in him" (John 9:3).

Ultimately the church has always found the larger meaning of sickness in the sufferings and death of Jesus.[19] Paul spells out this connection: "heirs of God, heirs with Christ, if only we suffer with him so as to be glorified with him. I consider the sufferings of the present to be as nothing compared with the glory to be revealed in us" (Rom. 8:17–18). In contrast with the naive enthusiasm of some Christian contemporaries, Paul firmly situates Christian living within the theology of the cross and draws out the corollaries of the presence of the Spirit within the church: we will be led on the same path as Christ.[20] The cross of Christ is the ultimate limit-experience that reveals the covenant compassion of God for his people.

Simply stated, the sick have a vocation. Again, the Pauline teaching is used to clarify this belief: "We should struggle against all sickness and carefully seek the blessings of good health, so that we can fulfill our role in human society and in the Church. Yet we should always be prepared to fill up what is lacking in Christ's sufferings for the salvation of the world."[21] For two thousand years the church has confronted the mystery of suffering with the mystery of the cross. The Christian disciple once more becomes an apprentice in exploring, through the disorienting experience of sickness, the meaning of Christ's giving of himself. This teaching is symbolized in the simple ritual of sprinkling the sick person with holy water and praying: "Let this water call to mind your baptismal sharing in Christ's redeeming passion and resurrection."[22]

This is a theology that can be eloquently preached, but only with effort realized and appropriated in the life of a suffering Christian.

Pastoral care has the difficult task of translating this theory into a praxis that will invite the participation of the sick and of the whole Christian community.

## The Mission to Heal

Luke presents the evocative scene of Jesus sending the Twelve out on mission: "He sent them forth to proclaim the reign of God and heal the afflicted" (Luke 9:2). The two tasks are complementary and faithfully reflect what Jesus himself did.[23] Healing in the Christian sense would have little meaning without the context of the good news of God's reign.

In the history of the church, as already mentioned, this ministry to the sick has been shared in many ways by Christians—religious nurses and doctors, Knights Hospitalers, pious associations for home visitation of the sick, and priests. But the new rites emphasize the communal responsibility of the church: "All Christians should share in the care and love of Christ and the Church for the sick and should show their concern for them, as much as each is able, by visiting them and comforting them in the Lord, offering them fraternal help in their need."[24] This ecclesial dimension has been given a practical pastoral form—the communal anointing of the sick.

Large segments of a parish may remain unaware of the extent and variety of sickness in their midst. The communal anointing of the sick, then, is as important for the healthy as for the ill. Such celebrations sensitize Christians to the needs of others, call in question their sense of service, and invite them to pray for others. The sick in the parish are a powerful symbol resonating the gospel questions that most Christians would rather avoid. In celebrating with the sick the proclamation of the gospel is heard and seen in new ways.

But in an early description of anointing of the sick the crucial question of faith is stated: "Is there anyone sick among you? He should ask for the presbyters of the church. They in turn are to pray over him, anointing him with oil in the Name (of the Lord). This prayer uttered in faith will reclaim the one who is ill, and the Lord will restore him to health" (James 5:14–15). While this passage is usually cited to illustrate an early form of ministry and one of its services, the crucial phrase is "this prayer uttered in faith." As the new ritual notes, the faith of both the minister and the recipient is important.[25]

The root of such faith and the power of the sacrament are found in the death and resurrection of Christ. But, as in all questions of faith and its sacramental expression, the promise of the kingdom also gives a future orientation to the present moment.[26] The pastoral care of the sick receives its direction from the gospel promise; "prayer uttered in faith" helps us welcome again the promise of God's kingdom. Many of the sick whom the pastoral minister encounters may have an undeveloped or unappropriated faith. In time of crisis, such as sickness, their natural reaction is to seek sacramental comfort and reassurance, but not necessarily to enter more deeply into the meaning of this event in their life, or into the gospel invitation to renewed discipleship. How does the pastoral minister respect the difficult situation of the people and yet challenge them?

The long-range objective of pastoral care in this matter, as in other sacramental situations, is to enable Christians to believe more deeply so that they may symbolize more honestly. This is all the more true in the Roman Catholic tradition, which ministers sacramentally more than some of the other Christian churches. It is of little pastoral value to preach, teach, and celebrate the anointing of the sick if the practical connections between faith and sacrament are not being explored. Throughout this book and elsewhere, I have argued for the pastoral importance of helping Christians to make seminal connections between their experience and their faith.[27]

When we see how the dying Francis of Assisi welcomed "Sister Death," the Christian ideal of a centered life leading through sickness to a meaningful death is dramatically concretized. What is easily forgotten is that Francis, like other great Christian saints, found the action of God in his own reflected experience. Augustine remembering his mother, Monica's, last illness, like Francis of Assisi and Ignatius of Loyola recalling their convalescence as young soldiers, reexamined familiar experience only to discover the unsettling demands of change and new meaning in the present.

Faith, in other words, deals with specific people, their communities, and their situations. God's initiation and continuing love does not encounter an anonymous humankind in a void, but rather is traced in the unique stories of first-name people. While pastoral care acknowledges this in principle, in praxis it may not always act on this basic insight. If pastoral care does not teach people to deal more insightfully with their own experience, how can they be expected to bring new meaning and commitment to the events of their lives, such as sickness, and to symbolize God's meaning sacramentally?

When the sick participate in the sacrament of anointing, they symbolize their faith and experience in response to the saving action of Christ. The unique value of a symbolic action is its ability to clarify our faith and experience and to stretch our horizons. In other words, persons who symbolize must intend what they are doing. Intention is the focus and meaning we give to our life and its actions. In the case of Christian symbols, the sacramental participant must intend what the church intends—to obey Christ's mandate to proclaim and live the gospel, and thus to prepare for the reign of God. To have such an intention is to move beyond the narrow confines of our own interests.

But such intentions require a starting point—our own experience. If sick persons are to arrive at deeper meaning, with the help of the symbolic anointing and prayer of the church, they must bring to the present situation past meanings derived from their personal story. Some examples might be helpful. Both Francis of Assisi and Ignatius of Loyola in their sickness had occasion to reassess the goals and meanings that had motivated their lives up to that point. Although both men had received sacraments many times before, their changing intention or life focus began in turn to reshape their participation in sacramental symbols. Thérèse of Lisieux's last sickness, though painful in many respects, helped to synthesize the ideals and values that had motivated her entry into religious life. Thérèse's reception of the sacraments in this final stage of her life assumed a new depth of meaning because her intentions had been clarified on the occasion of her final illness. By the way in which she saw God's action in her life at this point, Thérèse also perceived a new way in which to serve others.

Although the priest ministers the actual anointing, all Christians can participate in different ways in this ministry to the sick. Teaching the family, friends, and nursing staff how to enter into this ministry is still a neglected form of pastoral care. These are the people who have shared some of the experience of the sick, and who sometimes are in the best position to help the sick interpret and measure the meaning of past chapters of their life in view of the present. In effect, this is a practical application of the limit-experience and limit-expression mentioned earlier. From the vantage point of that which is unexpected or unwanted in their life, the sick can learn to speak the language of faith in a more authentic way.

The ritual's remarks about the prayer of the sick suggest the pastoral application: "The sick should be encouraged to pray when they are alone or with their families, friends, or those who care for them. Their prayer should draw primarily upon the scriptures, by meditating on those parts which speak of the mystery of human suffering in Christ. . . . The sick should be helped in making this sort of prayer, and priests should always be ready to pray with them."[28] The prayer of the sick and their communities can be revelatory if their need and God's Word coalesce into a new request for the gift of the Holy Spirit, who is constantly mentioned in the ritual. The Spirit strengthens and renews the whole person "so that he/she may be restored to your service."[29] And it is this same Spirit who attends to our unknown redemptive weakness and intercedes for us (Rom. 8:26–27).

## The Role of the Sick

Since the first Pentecost the gift of the Spirit has involved the anointing of Christians for the same purpose as Christ was anointed—the service of others. But even a casual walk through a busy hospital might make this theological understanding seem unrealistic. If anything, the complicated technological advances in medicine and the interpersonal professional problems of health care personnel sometimes seem to reduce the sick to passive recipients rather than people who have a new role to assume.

This role is succinctly stated in the ritual of anointing and care of the sick: "The role of the sick in the Church is to remind others not to lose sight of the essential or higher things and so to show that our mortal life is restored through the mystery of Christ's death and resurrection."[30] This role can perhaps best be examined through the eyes of the visitor to the sick. In medieval Europe lepers were kept on the fringes of society, but care of the ordinary sick was still done mainly at home. In Western society today serious illness is more often treated in hospitals. We have grown less accustomed to dealing directly with the sick. In other words, the sick are a symbol which often makes us uneasy, for they are a forceful reminder of our own mortality and limits. Sickness destroys many of the illusions entertained by a consumer society. Maintaining one's health and fighting illness are important objectives,[31] but the complementary role of the sick must also be developed in a society such as ours.

This complementary role can best be illustrated by a recent television documentary on the story of several cancer patients. The camera followed these people through lengthy periods of treatment until their death. The reactions of family, friends, medical personnel, and the sick themselves were carefully noted. The program is reported to have had a powerful effect on viewers throughout the country. The reasons for this success are not hard to find.

First, the reactions of the sick differed sharply. Some found new meaning for their life in the approach of death. They discovered important mentoring roles in teaching other sick persons how to cope with pain and despair, and in comforting their own circle of loved ones. Their experience supported the validity of Erik Erikson's insight into the nature of "true change" as a matter of "worthwhile conflict": "For it leads through the painful consciousness of one's position to a new conscience in that position."[32] Because these terminally ill people could face their own limits, they taught others to reassess and to stretch beyond their current goals and meanings. In contrast, other cancer patients portrayed in the TV documentary lost the will to live, because death itself was meaningless.

Second, both family and medical staff were affected—either negatively or positively—by the reaction of the sick. If the patient learned to cope with the illness in a positive way, then the family, doctors, and nurses were assisted in dealing with their own feelings and assessing their role in this life-crisis of another. On the other hand, the effect of the unmotivated or poorly coping sick persons on their surroundings was dramatically obvious in the documentary.

In brief, the gospel message about the meaning of life, death, and the kingdom of God, as concretized in Christ, is tested by the witness of a suffering Christian. Pastoral care should be able to assist this Christian to give a witness that will verify Paul's teaching: "We do not lose heart, because our inner being is renewed each day even though our body is being destroyed at the same time. The present burden of our trial is light enough, and earns for us an eternal weight of glory beyond all comparison. We do not fix our gaze on what is seen but on what is unseen. What is seen is transitory; what is unseen lasts forever" (2 Cor. 4:16–18).

### The Sick in the New Creation

For the Christian a discussion of sickness from the viewpoint of pastoral care must begin with a theology of creation and continue with a theology of the new creation in Christ.[33] The Christian learns to discover the creative love of God in the cyclic building up and tearing down that is part of all plant, animal, and human life. The experience of being a creature, a part of God's creation, is always potentially revelatory for we begin to realize the difference between God and ourselves, between his gift and our freedom. As Karl Rahner has pointed out, we cannot appreciate our freedom before God apart from our dependence upon him.[34] But this is a lesson we learn only with difficulty.

This is why Paul's teaching on a new creation in Christ is so radical in its implications: "This means that if anyone is in Christ, he is a new creation. The old order has passed away; now all is new! All this has been done by God, who has reconciled us to himself through Christ and has given us the ministry of reconciliation" (2 Cor. 5:17–18). In other words, though the building up and tearing down of creation continues, a totally new possibility for God's creation within us has arisen. Humans can deal with their experience in such a way that they will ultimately be able to welcome God's ultimate gift, his kingdom. For the Christian there is no growth and responsibility apart from the ongoing experience of this new creation in Christ.[35] Instead of using life-experience as an excuse for not finding God in his world and not participating actively in the new creation of Christ, Christian men and women begin to find God in their world and in the various shapes of their own experience.

Sickness is not simply a part of the tearing down process of creation. There is a theological insight in the popular usage that speaks of sickness as a cross. Only because of Christ's cross is there a new creation. Christians who are sick experience their dependence on God and their independence to choose whether they will be participants in Christ's mission and ministry. In a sense the sick Christian is invited to follow a path that other Christians have blazed.

Paul, referring to what may have been some sort of chronic sickness, recalls what he learned: " 'My grace is enough for you, for in weakness power reaches perfection.' And so I willingly boast of my weaknesses instead, that the power of Christ may rest upon me" (2 Cor. 12:9).[36] Twelve hundred years later another Christian, Francis of Assisi, struggled through his own sickness and found God's creation pointing toward the new creation. In his *Canticle of Brother Sun,* after praising God for a creation we take for granted, he prays: "All praise be yours, my Lord, through those who grant pardon for love of you; through those who endure sickness and trial. Happy those who endure in peace, by you they will be crowned."[37] These are but two examples of people whose limit-experiences resulted in limit-expressions of praise for God's new creation in their own lives.

Sickness, then, can be seen as another form of the catechumenal process. The familiar Word of God resonates in the ears of the sick with a challenge not heard before. As in the case of the catechumen, sick Christians must find new purpose if they are to continue to participate in God's new creation. Just as the church has traditionally described the catechumenal passage as one from darkness to light, so the Christian who is ill is asked and enabled to make the difficult transition from fear and self-pity to Paul's insight that Christ was "crucified out of weakness, but he lives by the power of God. We too are weak in him, but we live with him by God's power in us" (2 Cor. 13:4).

A theology of new creation, lived out in a catechumenal effort, provides fresh direction for pastoral care. A pastoral care of the weak that is ecclesially rooted and kingdom-oriented will be theologically guided in at least three respects.

First, pastoral care will enable the sick to find a gospel-comfort that includes new meaning. Such care will be different from the type of crisis counseling that simply enables people to recognize and vent feelings but can give no new orientation for this turning point in the person's life. "Comfort" in its root sense means "to strengthen," and should not be confused with a spiritual palliative. The ritual recognizes this need: "The person who is seriously ill needs the special help of God's grace in this time of anxiety, lest he/she be broken in spirit and subject to temptations and weakening of faith. Christ, therefore, strengthens the faithful who are afflicted by illness with the sacrament of anointing, providing them with the strongest means of support."[38]

But people cannot arrive at new meanings in their life by simply bypassing the old meanings. Evangelization of the sick, therefore, that does not involve a complementary invitation to discern how God's action has been traced out in prior and present experience, is pastorally truncated. On the other hand, when Christians are helped to struggle with the real forces that have shaped their lives, then the resulting prayer reaches beyond solace to ask for the strength and light promised in the anointing of the sick.

Second, the sacramental dimension of the pastoral care of the sick is clarified by the way in which the sacraments of initiation are prepared for in the catechumenal process. Unlike Christians who are baptized in infancy, adult catechumens are in penance for the forgiveness of sin long before they receive baptism for the remission of sins. The anointing of the sick always includes this penitential dimension: "May the Lord who frees you from sin save you and raise you up."[39] The evangelization process just described gives new edge to the familiar avowal, "I have sinned through my own fault."

Baptism and anointing with chrism—not to mention the Eucharist as well—are sacraments of initiation that derive their full meaning within their traditional context of the catechumenate. They are intensive and highly coded symbols of the death, resurrection, and mission of Christ. As these sacraments are celebrated in the catechumenal context of the Easter vigil, the Christian community surrounds the neophytes and participates with them in the shared meanings of the Christ-event.

In brief, the ecclesial nature of these sacraments, with their powerful call for service to Christ's gospel, is an important element in the administration of the sacraments to the sick. Contrast this traditional theology and praxis, for example, with some vestiges of a different sacramental praxis in which the Eucharist is quickly given to patients in a two-hundred-bed hospital or in a large parish.

Third and finally, pastoral care announces the kingdom of God to the sick in such a way that the present time is prized for the sake of others. In the manual theology prior to Vatican II seminarians always studied a section of systematic theology called "The Last Things." Since Vatican II some key perspectives have been restored to this theology, including an awareness of how the reality of God's kingdom already begun among us radically changes our sense of death and judgment. An authentic eschatology always transforms the way in which we choose to live out the present responsibly and to perceive death in the light of Good Friday and Easter Sunday.

Current counseling of the seriously ill includes empathetic support that can enable them to deal with their fear of death. But pastoral care must do more than that. If the initial experience of God's kingdom is already among us, then we expect to find indications of it in our shared and personal experience. Perhaps "the last things" sometimes seem unreal in our preaching and praxis because we have not helped Christians to locate God's future in their past and present experience. Emily Dickinson's ironic comment in one of her poems should call in question our pastoral proclamation of this good news: "Going to heaven . . . how dim it sounds!"

## YOUTH MINISTRY

A major concern in pastoral care today—along with care of the sick—is youth ministry. The concern is not new. Why, then, does not the Catholic Youth Organization, the Newman Club, or even the extensive Catholic school system have the same pastoral effectiveness today as it had two or three decades ago? The answer is fairly obvious: rapid cultural, political, and psychological changes have had a profound effect on the growing young person. The upheavals of the sixties in the United States and the revolution in France in 1968 are but two examples of this profound unrest among youth. Over the past decade the proliferation of cult groups seeking to attract young people has deeply concerned parents and the church.

Vatican II reflected on such phenomena: "A change in attitudes and in human structures frequently calls accepted values into question. This is especially true of young people who have grown impatient on more than one occasion, and indeed become rebels in distress."[40]

Youth exerts such a far-reaching influence on society that it is hard adequately to evaluate its impact.[41] Often enough this influence of youth on society has a boomerang effect on youth; it tends to destroy some of the traditional societal supports for youth. Current cultural and social expectations impose a heavy burden on the young in ways that their parents did not know. The post–Vatican II church too, in this nuclear age menaced by worldwide problems of hunger, injustice, and destruction, has greater expectations of its young.[42]

Vatican II assigned no easy task when it asked priests to give special attention to youth.[43] The council itself acknowledged that overcoming the age barrier between generations and recognizing the social environment in which youth must grow up are necessary but difficult first steps for those who would interact with young people.[44] But what is not noted often enough is that this same council called youth to active ministry within the church. Older Christians are to be, for the young, a model of mission. In the same vein, a major thesis of this book has been that an evangelical pastoral care must evoke a commitment to mission from all Christians. A crucial test of this thesis is today's youth ministry.

## Zeal and Mission

The praxis of pastoral care among the young does not always honor this mission imperative of the council. A dichotomized approach to youth is one symptom of the problem. At St. Joseph's parish, for example, the youth minister effectively gathers teenagers for social and religious activities, such as the "Search" weekend. He has also started a small but active group of young adults. This humanizing dimension of pastoral care is juxtaposed to a sacramental care of youth that is sometimes post–Vatican II in ritual but preconciliar in praxis.

The current catechetical debate on Confirmation within the Roman Catholic church is another example of the problem. Is Confirmation a sacrament for ten-year-olds or is it the Christian rite of passage for teenagers and young adults? Or is this perhaps the wrong question to be asking about the sacrament? At St. Joseph's, in any case, the praxis definition of mission is being shaped in part by the way in which this question is handled.

As any trained youth minister knows, the question of Confirmation cannot be solved if the discussion is limited to chronological age groups. "Youth" is a broad term that can cover more than one stage of life and is defined more by crisis and change than by birthdays. The praxis of Confirmation, then, is a practical pastoral way in which we deal with the complex theological question of how much can be expected of youth in terms of mission within the church.[45] The larger ecclesial question is whether St. Joseph's has any perceived need for the mission of its youth.

The modest aim of this discussion is to apply once more— illustratively, with respect to teenage and young adult years—the guidelines derived from the theologically normative process of the catechumenate: What sort of inquiry should pastoral care encourage among the young? What peculiar obstacles do youth experience in trying to clarify their intentions as growing Christian people? Does the nuclear-age society allow any place for the mission of young Christians? To attempt to answer such questions is to take seriously Vatican II's belief that as the youth become "more conscious of their own personality, they are impelled by a zest for life and abounding energies to assume their own responsibility, and they yearn to play their part in social and cultural life. If this zeal is imbued with the spirit of Christ and is inspired by obedience to and love for the shepherds of the Church, it can be expected to be very fruitful."[46]

## Rebellious Inquiry

In commenting on a saying attributed to Thomas Jefferson, Erikson says: "Jefferson . . . once said . . . 'God forbid that we should ever be twenty years without . . . a rebellion.' Why twenty years? Did he, maybe, refer not only to history but also to the life cycle: God forbid anybody should be twenty years old without having rebelled?"[47] Erikson's contention is that it takes about twenty years of development to possess an identity that energizes action realistically and utilizes the past creatively. He situates adolescence and the young adult years as stages five and six in human development. The success with which young people deal with the challenges of these stages directly affects their sense of purpose and the realism of their symbols.

The gospel calls youth to a conversion within a covenant community forged by the shared commitment to Christ's way. But this call is heard within a dynamic period of transition in the young person's life. The problem is illustrated by the very definition that Erikson gives for identity: "a sense of being at one with oneself as one grows and develops; and it means, at the same time, a sense of affinity with a community's sense of being at one with its future as well as its history."[48] Where youth are concerned, community includes not only the familial and social groups but the church community as well. The church understands itself much as in Erikson's definition—as the community that proclaims God's future in such a way as to transform the present. But does the church contribute to the identity of youth?

Erikson, in a series of broad strokes, has etched the tensive qualities of adolescence: the abandonment of the familiar, the search for ideals to live by, the need for vigorous meaning, the importance of the choice of occupation for identity, and the search for sexual identity.[49] But the key strength that Erikson identifies as requisite for this stage of adolescence is fidelity: "The ability to sustain loyalties freely pledged in spite of the inevitable contradictions of value systems."[50]

Youth's struggle for fidelity clarifies their complementary search for a broader view of the world and their place in it.[51] In attempting to honor important loyalties, the young person can often experience the confusion occasioned by conflicting roles and relationships. A dramatic and complex example is afforded by the protest movement against the Vietnam War in the sixties. The expectations of parents and of youthful peer groups often clashed. Many young Americans sensed a lack of moral leadership on the part of their religious and political leaders. Growing up in the sixties included, in addition to the usual adolescent maturation problems, the larger social and religious questions of loyalty, pitched in a difficult key. The way in which the young are willing to take a hard look at the world that lies beyond their own doorstep directly shapes the quality of their maturity, their commitments, and their sense of faith.

We cannot expect young people to strive for an appropriated faith apart from these wider social and cultural contexts. If in the obedience of faith, as Vatican II so beautifully taught, a person "entrusts his/her whole self freely to God" in response to his/her initiating and saving action, then the contexts which shape or deform "the whole self" of the young will have to be taken more seriously.[52] The human sciences forcefully remind the theologian and the youth minister that "the whole self" is a more complex reality than our theories and ministries might sometimes indicate. Pastoral care of youth is certainly not an attempt to help youth achieve some theoretical advance in terms of Erikson's stages of life or James Fowler's stages of faith.[53] But the value of such theoretical work is the prophetic questioning it provides about our ministry and its goals.

What roles and relations does the church community, in the name of the gospel, ask of the young person? Change and meaning are certainly defined in more demanding terms in the gospel than in Erikson. For young Christians with their fragmented self-awareness Paul issues a difficult challenge: "Help carry one another's burdens; in that way you will fulfill the law of Christ. . . . Everyone should bear his own responsibility" (Gal. 6:2, 5). "You should live in accord with the spirit and you will not yield to the cravings of the flesh. . . . Those who belong to Christ Jesus have crucified their flesh with its passions and desires" (Gal. 5:16, 24). Such challenges resonate differently in the ears of an adolescent searching for sexual identity than in the ears of an adult who has already arrived at some sense of an integrated sexuality.

A practical pastoral corollary of this sensitivity to the social and cultural contexts in which youth must grow up is again the question of Confirmation. Sacraments are powerful symbols that enable us to maintain continuity with the risen Lord and his mission. The sacraments of initiation, as we have seen, situate the individual Christian's faith within the mission of the ecclesial community. Confirmation, as part of this initiation process, cannot be discussed apart from that mission.

But the church's mission today is carried out in even more complicated contexts than that of the Roman Empire of the second century or the feudal society of the thirteenth century. By what tasks and roles does the contemporary church redefine mission in this century? The young Roman soldier, as we have seen, identified as a catechumen with the sense of mission imparted to him by the second-century church. The church attempted to define "growing up in Christ" in terms of the challenge of growing up in the Roman Empire, with all its attendant obstacles to gospel-living.

Erikson's description of how the community confirms the identity of young people is borne out: "Identity thus is not the sum of childhood identifications, but rather a new combination of old and new identification fragments. For this very reason societies *confirm* an individual at this time in all kinds of ideological frameworks and assign roles and tasks to him in which he can *recognize* himself and *feel recognized*. Ritual confirmations, initiations, and indoctrinations only enhance an indispensable process by which healthy societies bestow traditional strength on the new generation and thereby bind to themselves the strength of youth."[54]

In other words, the church must confirm and indeed radicalize the gospel message in ways that will be challenging to youth, and to which youth can respond. The teaching of John XXIII, Paul VI, and John Paul II, for example, on social and economic justice and on nuclear armaments affords an example. This teaching attempts to interpret the gospel call to conversion in terms of the contemporary world in which we must live out our faith. Catechumenal evangelization in turn invites inquiry of young people about these issues in such a way that commitments can be made and the significance of the anointing of the Spirit correctly focused. In trying to contextualize Confirmation in such ways, pastoral care helps young people to be honest and motivated in what they intend in these rituals.[55] These efforts in no way detract from the gratuitous action of Christ that is the root of all faith and sacrament. Rather such care assists young Christians to participate in the transforming purpose of sacrament.

### Sexuality and Intimacy

If teenagers are to arrive at an integrated awareness of self and others by their young adult years, a crucial test will be the matter of intimacy—"the capacity to commit himself to concrete affiliations and partnerships and to develop the ethical strength to abide by such commitments, even though they call for significant sacrifices and compromises."[56] "Intimacy," as Erikson uses the term, includes the integration of genital sexuality into an awareness of self and others that enables the young adult to be committed and responsible in relationships.

In pre–Vatican II days a major pastoral concern in dealing with youth had to do with specific sexual activities, such as masturbation and petting. Although purity was proposed as a positive ideal, pastoral effort and teaching were directed primarily to helping young people avoid sexual practices and daydreaming. The result was that the confessions of young people often tended to concentrate on sexual sin, thus reinforcing a negative sexual awareness. The post–Vatican II church has not changed its realistic pastoral view that a selfish sexuality impairs a person's ability both to relate to God and others and to commit oneself for the sake of others. But announcing the gospel's challenge to unselfish embodiment and responsible sexuality within the positive framework of Christian love is the privileged task of pastoral care.

Paul, for example, contrasts "lewd conduct, impurity, licentiousness, . . . orgies" (Gal. 5:19, 21)—examples of being of "the flesh," embracing a distorted life style and value system that ultimately excludes God—with "the fruit of the spirit . . . love, joy, peace, patient endurance, kindness, generosity, faith, mildness, and chastity" (Gal. 5:22–23). "Spirit" in Paul's language is a positive ideal that motivates the Christian to change selfish life styles and values.

As never before, young people need to hear the gospel call to sexual intimacy within a positive theology of love that is credible and relevant. Tertullian's insight that "the flesh is the hinge of salvation" is correct in ways that he himself could not appreciate.[57] For the doctrine of creation which sees the embodied person as good leads to the doctrine of salvation in which the resurrection of the body is a powerful symbol of God's total redemption of what he has lovingly created.[58]

If youth ministry is to fulfill its task of proclaiming the good news to maturing people, it must take seriously the complexities of human intimacy and sexuality in the light of developmental studies. The Christian teachings on creation and redemption come alive, for example, when understood in terms of responsible and embodied awareness of the other as person (and not simply in terms of gender), of an appropriate tactility at each stage of life in ritualizing relationships, of an incipient generativity (Erikson's "knowing how to care for what we create") which can symbolize care and tenderness in responsible ways,[59] and of rich celibacy that is not to be confused simply with the life of unmarried people. After all, Paul's invitation to "greet one another with a holy kiss" (2 Cor. 13:12) has been ritualized in the kiss of peace for nearly two thousand years. This symbol captures the gospel ideal that the embodied affection and mutuality of Christians already anticipates the reign of God wherein shared intimacy and presence will be among the final fruits of the Spirit.

If, on the other hand, the church in its pastoral care and teaching cannot better contextualize and proclaim the gospel call to unselfish sexuality and credible intimacy, then Christian youth may have to achieve the generativity necessary for their adult years despite the church. This would be a loss for all concerned. Examples are not hard to find. In 1967 a play by one of France's great literary figures, Henri de Motherlant, caused a sensation. *The City Whose Prince is a Child* deals with particular friendships among boys at a Catholic boarding school. But the dramatic action in Motherlant's play is centered around the attitudes toward sexuality and intimacy on the part of two priests. In the final confrontation the older priest says: "Yes, our religion is founded on love. . . . When it attains a certain degree of the absolute, by its intensity, perennial quality, and self-lessness, it is close to the love of God."[60] Yet the context of the play's ᵗory betrays a theology of love and sexuality that is paralyzed by guilt and fear, and can never retrieve a positive sense of embodiment and love. Pastoral care in these waning years of the twentieth century should have much more to teach today's youth than this theological caricature of a Christian love so suspect and disembodied.

## MINISTRY TO THE ELDERLY

One of the dramatic scenes of the Acts of the Apostles involves the ecstatic experience of the disciples on Pentecost and Peter's justification of it from the prophet Joel: "I will pour out a portion of my spirit on all mankind: your sons and daughters shall prophesy, your young men shall see visions and your old men shall dream dreams" (Acts 2:17). Erikson, to my knowledge, has never alluded to the line, but he would heartily approve of the thought. The adolescent and young adult years must include ecstatic and visionary components which motivate youth to see the wonders of God's work and to participate in it. But the complementary dreams of the old are equally important for they capture the future in the present.

A major concern of pastoral care is centered on people in the last decades of their life. In fact, pastoral care of the elderly today probably takes up a more significant proportion of pastoral effort than ever before. In the twentieth century life expectancy has taken a quantum leap from forty-seven to seventy-three years of age. With this expanded life span new challenges to pastoral care have also arisen. Unfortunately, the brevity of Vatican II's passing allusion to this challenge does not mirror its importance: "The livelihood and the human dignity of those especially who are in particularly difficult circumstances because of illness or old age should be safeguarded."[61]

Daniel Levinson graphically sums up the situation: "An American man's sense of what it means to be young or old is shaped by the cultural symbols and images, by the schools and occupations, by the realities and meanings of Medicare, retirement, social security, Florida condominiums, death and dying. . . . It is hard to integrate the Young/Old polarity in the self when the external world draws such a hard line between Young and Old and makes it so frightening to be other than young."[62]

### Integrity and Meaning

As anyone in pastoral care ministry knows, questions of health, loneliness, safety, a sense of purpose, the use of leisure and relations between young and old are not secular problems; rather, they form a crucial test of being Christian at sixty-seven or seventy-five years of age. Senior citizens' clubs and hot lunches for the elderly are hardly a pastoral panacea for these deeper threats.

Erikson long ago put his finger on the key issue: "Any span of the [life] cycle lived without vigorous meaning, at the beginning, in the middle, or at the end, endangers the sense of life and the meaning of death in all whose life stages are intertwined."[63] The strength of Erikson's insight is that he shows the interrelation of the young and old as grounded in this question of meaning: Why was I and why am I still here?

It will repay both the theologian and those who work in pastoral care to reread some of Erikson's broad but acute observations about the last life-stage. If an adult has tried to work through the challenge and crisis of being a generative person, there remains the final riddle of the Sphinx—the question of integrity. The word derives from the Latin *integer* (meaning "whole") and summarizes the effort to make our life whole. We view our lives from a new vantage point and judge whether it was worth living. We reassess relationships and their mutual impact. We regret and we rejoice.

Retirement, after all, is a rite of passage, and often enough the occasion of crisis for many people. It can provide the possibility of a leisure which is either wanted or unwelcome. It can afford the possibility either of deepening a relationship or of frankly acknowledging that that relationship has long since died. The attitudes with which people cope in this last stage may range from mature to passive or even angry.[64] But what is ultimately striking about this period is the finality of choices and decisions that are made. Failure to find "vigorous meaning" in one's life at this point can justify an anger or despair that substitutes rituals for dreams and bitterness for hope. When there are no prophets among the old, then the new Israel—the church—is the poorer. Or, to return to Erikson's thought, "healthy children will not fear life if their elders have integrity enough not to fear death."[65]

### Experience and Religion

For the Christian, old age can be most deceptive of all the stages of life. Several dimensions of the religious perception and experience of the elderly need to be distinguished.[66] The experiential or feeling ˙mension of the faith life of older people has been shaped by a long ᵗory of training and use. Catholic piety of the pre–Vatican II ᵒd placed great emphasis on devotional practices—such as ben- ᵒn of the Blessed Sacrament, first Fridays, rosary, stations of ˙ss, novenas—that had a strong affective component. While this dimension has not disappeared, it has sometimes taken other expressions. Any pastoral minister who has assisted at the communal anointing of the sick or communal penitential rites can testify to the strong affective dimension of these celebrations for some elderly people.

But these same celebrations contain another important dimen sion—ritualism. The ritualistic ways in which the anointing of t sick or the Eucharist are celebrated also resonate, for better worse, with the religious feelings and attitudes of people. danger is that the affective and the ritualistic elements in celebrations will be juxtaposed but not integrated. An example, as the Eucharist, might concretize the problem. Many elderly p find consolation, peace, and similar affective meanings th their participation in the Eucharist. The rituals of this sacram supposed to help them enter into the religious meaning of a that proclaims the death of the Lord until he comes (1 Cor When the religious feelings of the participants do not ben the religious meaning of the Eucharist, a major pastoral arises.[67] The pastoral idea that "the law of worship is belief" is in praxis not being realized. Privatized meaning

In our post–Vatican II era the connection between s care and the religious affections of older Christians is a but neglected area of pastoral care. With the major conc of the past two decades many older Christians hav become disoriented. Former religious meanings an have been joined to compliance with new rituals, bu tion has not always resulted in the kind of enriched r standing that can elicit a more profound affective re words, Eucharist in the Pauline sense as commun forming death and resurrection for the Christia rich and integrating source of meaning for the ol challenge to pastoral care is to assist these Christia powerful sacramental symbols in which they pa priate their own strong feelings about commur

One element of this pastoral assistance is o Many older Christians have never heard ade how faith and sacramental experience can particular difficulties of their stage of life. working out of a preconciliar theology that directions and emphases of the postconcilia gogical point of view it is revelatory for old many of the ritual changes are a restorati liturgical praxis. It is even more enlightening for them to discover that there are sometimes more relevant and understandable theological explanations of the central mysteries of faith than those out of which they currently operate.

A second element of pastoral assistance is moral. It is not uncommon for a confessor to hear an older person say, "Well, Father, at my age what can you really do wrong?" Erikson might reply, "You can stagnate; you can despair." To have a Christian sense of morality in the last stage of life demands more of a person than at any previous stage. But the demands are subtle and elusive. The radical temptation of our final years is to lose a sense of purpose and of being "for the sake of others." More than at any other stage the final moral stance of the elderly is judged by their positive awareness, and not simply by their avoidance of sinful actions. Erikson's "new conscience," it will be remembered, is the result of struggling to be aware of our limits and our gifts, carried in earthen vessels.[68]

The catechumenal guidelines suggested at the beginning of this chapter also apply here. The final stages of conversion elicit the deepest need for inquiry on the part of older people concerning God's action in the prior chapters of their lives, and its meaning for the final chapter. The intentions of the elderly are crucial, for they once more stretch self-made limits and suggest new possibilities and purposes. When we look at some outstanding older Christians—Vincent de Paul, Dorothy Day, Mother Teresa of Calcutta—we are again reminded of Paul's promise of new being in Christ. Inquiry and intention are key elements of this Pauline newness.

The sacraments of the elderly do heal them for service and for mission as long as they have life. Here is where the Christian relation between the young and the old is perhaps best demonstrated. Youth must have credible models of lived meaning that permit and inspire hope-filled death. The young/old polarity in our society leads, if anything, to a denial of death that robs life of meaning. With some notable exceptions, pastoral care has yet to find ways in which the young and the old can once more learn from one another the cost and the joy of being Christian.

## POST-EASTER LESSONS

When theologians write of pastoral care, the mildly skeptical reaction of those who minister is understandable. Safely removed from the humdrum and banal details of pastoral care, so the reasoning goes, the theologian sets up constructs and proposes lines of action that he or she does not have to implement. While there is a measure of truth in this objection, it is also true that whenever theology has dialogued with praxis both have been the richer for it.

Theology at its best does not speak of utopian goals, but of God's work in the life of ordinary people. Theologians would be unfaithful if they did not believe that God makes the impossible possible, and that he alone heals where others have not yet seen the wound. In complementary ways people in pastoral care can testify to that same work and healing in their life and in the lives of others. But the shared task of theologians and pastoral care ministers is to make God's Word and work credible and visible in their time and culture.

A rich source of reflection for the discouraged theologian or minister of pastoral care is available in the post-Easter accounts of the New Testament. Here are the early Christian community's testimonies to the pastoral care of the risen Lord. In effect, the oral tradition that carried the stories of an unperceptive and denying Peter, and of a doubting Thomas, was implicitly asking, How could such people minister to others? The post-Resurrection accounts are the answer to that question. Theologies of pastoral care were first fashioned on the shores of the Sea of Tiberias when a risen Lord healed flawed people with his call "Come and eat your meal," and his challenge "Feed my lambs. . . . Tend my sheep" (John 21:1–18).

Good theological reflection invites those who work in pastoral care to stretch beyond the limits and frustrations of their working situations, to ask old questions with greater perception, and to pose new questions not asked before. Creative pastoral praxis unsettles the neat categories and formulations of the theologians and reminds them forcefully that God's enduring presence and saving action remain a mystery despite our most lucid comments. Properly chastened by God's Word, both theologian and pastoral care minister can learn from Francis of Assisi's summons to his brothers: "Let us begin again, for up to now we have made little or no progress."[69] The challenge is to "rebuild my house," and pastoral care for tomorrow will be—with the sick, youth, the elderly, and all to whom and with whom we minister—a participant in that rebuilding.

# Notes

## INTRODUCTION

1. Georges Bernanos, *The Diary of a Country Priest,* trans. P. Morris (New York: Macmillan Co., 1937).
2. Heinz Schuster, *Sacramentum Mundi,* s.v. "Pastoral Theology."

## CHAPTER 1

1. Pastoral theology has typically been defined as "a science that discusses the duties, obligations, and opportunities *of the priest* in the care of souls and proposes the means of success in his work" (James G. Brennan, "Pastoral Theology," *New Catholic Encyclopedia,* 10: 1080; emphasis added.) For a current survey of the "priestly-sacramental" component of ministry, see *Ministry in America,* ed. Merton P. Strommen, David S. Schuller, Milo L. Brekke (New York: Harper & Row, 1980), 45–46, 481–82.
2. Don Browning, *The Moral Context of Pastoral Care* (Philadelphia: Westminster Press, 1976), 14. Under the influence of social-critical theory, the nature, method, and goals of practical theology are being reexamined in Germany. See, for example, Rolf Zerfass, "Praktische Theologie als Handlungswissenschaft," in *Praktische Theologie Heute,* ed. Ferdinand Klostermann and R. Zerfass (Grünewald: Kaiser, 1974), 164–77; and Norbert Mette, "Praktische Theologie als Handlungswissenschaft," *Diakonia* 10 (1979): 190–203.
3. Browning, *Moral Context,* 14, 19–20; Heinz Schuster, *Sacramentum Mundi,* s.v. "Pastoral Theology."
4. Seward Hiltner, *Preface to Pastoral Theology* (Nashville: Abingdon Press, 1958), 20. The "shepherding" perspective, however, can be understood by Roman Catholics in a clerical sense; see James N. Lapsley, "Pastoral Theology Past and Present," in *The New Shape of Pastoral Theology,* ed. William B. Oglesby, Jr. (Nashville: Abingdon Press, 1969), 43.
5. William Clebsch and Charles Jaekle, *Pastoral Care in Historical Perspective* (Englewood Cliffs, N.J.: Prentice-Hall, 1964), 8–9.
6. Henri J. Nouwen, *Creative Ministry* (Garden City, N.Y.: Doubleday & Co., 1971).

7. John T. McNeill, *A History of the Cure of Souls* (New York: Harper & Brothers, 1951).

8. The themes are described in *Ministry in America*, 25–26. For a fuller development of some of the comments made here, see Regis A. Duffy, "A Theological Critique of the Professional Model of Ministry," *St. Luke's Journal of Theology* 25 (1982): 86–105.

9. For the complex background of this verse and its theology, see Ernst Käsemann, *Commentary on Romans*, Eng. trans. G. W. Bromiley (Grand Rapids: Wm. B. Eerdmans, 1978), 318–21.

10. Karl Rahner, *Foundations of Christian Faith* (New York: Crossroad, 1978), 20.

11. See, for example, "Decree on the Church's Missionary Activity" (*Ad Gentes*), par. 39 in *The Documents of Vatican II*, ed. W. M. Abbott (New York: Association Press, 1966), 627.

12. "Decree on the Apostolate of the Laity" (*Apostolicam Actuositatem*), par. 5 in *Documents*, 495. I have not corrected the exclusive male terminology in this published translation from the Latin.

13. "Decree on the Bishops' Pastoral Office in the Church" (*Christus Dominus*), par. 31 in *Documents*, 419.

14. "Decree on the Ministry and Life of Priests" (*Presbyterorum Ordinis*), par. 2 in *Documents*, 533–34 (emphasis added).

15. "Dogmatic Constitution on the Church" (*Lumen Gentium*), par. 10 in *Documents*, 27.

16. Joseph Komonchak, "Clergy, Laity, and the Church's Mission in the World," *The Jurist* 41 (1981): 439.

17. See David N. Power's discussion of the conciliar debate on this matter in *Ministers of Christ and His Church: The Theology of the Priesthood* (London: Geoffrey Chapman, 1969), 144–46.

18. David N. Power, *Gifts That Differ: Lay Ministries Established and Unestablished* (New York: Pueblo Publishing, 1980), 44–47.

19. See, for example, Vatican II's "Decree on Apostolate of Laity," par. 29: "Since laymen share in their own way in the mission of the Church, their apostolic formation takes its special flavor from the distinctively secular quality of the lay state and from its own form of spirituality" (*Documents*, 516–17).

20. *Documents*, 60.

21. Edward Kilmartin has pinpointed this problem in his excellent discussion, "Lay Participation in the Apostolate of the Hierarchy," *The Jurist* 41 (1981): 343–70.

22. Ibid., 352–57; see also, Edward C. Schillebeeckx's analysis of the 1971 Synod of Bishops position on ministry in *Ministry* (New York: Crossroad, 1981), 105–42.

23. For the larger theological issues behind the question of office in the church, see Edward C. Schillebeeckx, "The Christian Community and Its Office-Bearers," in *The Right of the Community to a Priest*, ed. E. Schillebeeckx

and Johann-Baptist Metz, Concilium 133 (New York: Seabury Press, 1980), 95–133.

24. *As One Who Serves: Reflections on the Pastoral Ministry of Priests in the United States* (Washington, D.C.: United States Catholic Conference, 1977), 45–46.

25. For the history and theology of the catechumenate see Michael Dujarier, *A History of the Catechumenate* (New York: William H. Sadlier, 1982); idem, *The Rite of Christian Initiation* (New York: William H. Sadlier, 1982); Raymond Kemp, *A Journey in Faith: An Experience of the Catechumenate* (New York: William H. Sadlier, 1979); William J. Reedy, ed., *Becoming a Catholic Christian* (New York: William H. Sadlier, 1978); Aidan Kavanagh, *The Shape of Baptism: The Rite of Christian Initiation* (New York: Pueblo Publishing, 1978), 126–49.

26. For a fuller discussion of the theological implications of this process, see Regis A. Duffy, *Real Presence: Worship, Sacraments, and Commitment* (New York: Harper & Row, 1982), 108–32.

27. See Victor Turner, *The Ritual Process: Structure and Anti-Structure* (Chicago: Aldine Publishing, 1969); idem, "Passages, Margins and Poverty: Religious Symbols of Communities," *Worship* 46 (1972): 390–412, 482–94.

28. Dujarier gives an interesting reference to a similar example in *History of Catechumenate*, 38.

29. See A. M. Carr-Saunders and P. A. Wilson, *Encyclopedia of the Social Sciences*, s.v. "Profession"; also, P. Elliott, *The Sociology of Professions* (New York: Herder & Herder, 1972), 2–11.

30. Elliott Krause, *The Sociology of Occupations* (Boston: Little, Brown & Co., 1971), 75.

31. Urban T. Holmes III, for example, has argued against this restricted notion of a professional model of ministry in several of his works: *The Priest in Community: Exploring the Roots of Ministry* (New York: Seabury Press, 1978), 71; *The Future Shape of Ministry* (New York: Seabury Press, 1971), 175–77; "Transcendence and Ministry," *Anglican Theological Review* 54 (1972): 3–20; *Ministry and Imagination* (New York: Seabury Press, 1976).

32. See, for example, Schillebeeckx, *Ministry*, 66–74, where he points out how Vatican II retained medieval notions of the "power of orders and of jurisdiction" and juxtaposed some of the early church's concept of ministry.

33. *Rite of Christian Initiation of Adults* (Washington, D.C.: United States Catholic Conference, 1974) was officially promulgated in 1972.

## CHAPTER 2

1. *The Governance of God*, bk. 6, c. 7, *The Writings of Salvian, the Presbyter*, Eng. trans. by Jeremiah F. O'Sullivan (New York: Fathers of the Church, 1947), 163.

2. Gabriel Le Bras, *Institutions ecclésiastiques de la Chrétienté médiévale*, vol. 12 of *Histoire de l'Eglise*, ed. Augustin Fliche and Victor Martin (Paris: Bloud et Gay, 1959), 140 and n. 8.

3. For a summary discussion see Carolyn Osiek, "Relation of Charism to Rights and Duties in the New Testament Church," *Jurist* 41 (1981): 301–2.

4. Käsemann, *Commentary on Romans*, 335.

5. John Meier, "Presbyteros in the Pastoral Epistles," *Catholic Biblical Quarterly* 35 (1973): 323–45; also, André Lemaire, *Les Ministères aux Origines de l'Eglise* (Paris: Cerf, 1971), 123–38.

6. Schillebeeckx, "Christian Community," 106–10; Hervé-Marie Legrand, "The Presidency of the Eucharist According to the Ancient Tradition," *Worship* 53 (1979): 413–38.

7. See Peter R. Brown's discussion in *Augustine of Hippo: A Biography* (Berkeley and Los Angeles: University of California Press, 1967), 194–97.

8. Bernard J. Cooke, *Ministry to Word and Sacraments: History and Theology* (Philadelphia: Fortress Press, 1976), 355; for a similar description of the changing role of priests in the early Middle Ages, see Friedrich Kempf et al., *The Church in the Age of Feudalism*, vol. 3 of *Handbook of Church History*, ed. H. Jedin (New York: Herder & Herder, 1969), 307–12, and Le Bras, *Institutions ecclésiastiques*, 150–71.

9. David N. Power points to the historical irony in a similar example in the East, with Basil's ascetic ideal for church office preparing the way for its clericalization; see "The Basis for Official Ministry in the Church," *The Jurist* 41 (1981): 326–27.

10. Gregory the Great, *Pastoral Care*, Eng. trans. by Henry Davis (Westminster, Md.: Newman Press, 1950), 21; emphasis added.

11. See James Moudry, "Bishop and Priest in the Sacrament of Holy Orders," in *Who Decides in the Church? Studies in Co-Responsibility*, ed. James A. Coriden (Hartford: Canon Law Society of America, 1971), 163–86.

12. G. Fransen, "The Tradition in Medieval Canon Law," in *The Sacrament of Holy Orders* (Collegeville, Minn.: Liturgical Press, 1962), 212; emphasis added.

13. Power, "Basis for Official Ministry," 331; emphasis added.

14. McNeill, *History of Cure of Souls*.

15. *On Penitence*, 6, in *Tertullian: Treatises on Penance*, Eng. trans. William Le Saint (Westminster, Md.: Newman Press, 1959), 24; emphasis added.

16. *On Penitence*, 7, in *Tertullian*, trans. Le Saint, 29; emphasis added.

17. See Cyrille Vogel, *Le Pécheur et la Pénitence dans l'Eglise Ancienne* (Paris: Cerf, 1966), 34.

18. See for example Augustine, *On the Gospel of St. John*, 4, 13 in *Nicene and Post-Nicene Fathers*, vol. 7 (New York: Charles Scribner's Sons, 1908), 29.

19. Sermon 67, in *Saint Caesarius of Arles: Sermons*, trans. Mary M. Mueller (New York: Fathers of the Church, 1956), 1: 318.

20. Sermon 60, in *St. Caesarius*, trans. Mueller, 1: 296.

21. Rule of St. Benedict, c. 46, in *The Rule of St. Benedict*, ed. Oswald H. Blair (Fort Augustus, Eng.: 1948), 121.

22. John T. McNeill and Helena Gamer, trans., *Medieval Handbooks of Penance* (New York: Octagon Books, 1965), 92.

23. Ibid., 144.

24. An Irish Collection of Canons, no. 37, in ibid., 141.

25. Thomas N. Tentler's *Sin and Confession on the Eve of the Reformation* (Princeton, N.J.: Princeton University, 1977) provides a generally accurate summary of this literature.

26. John Duns Scotus, IV *Sentences*, dist. 14, qu. 4, n. 2 (emphasis added) in *Omnia Opera* (Paris: Vives, 1894), 18: 139.

27. These discussions on the abuses of the sacrament of penance took place in August and November 1547, at the council. The minutes for these interesting sessions can be found in *Concilii Tridentini Actorum*, Partis Tertiae, volumen prius (Freiburg-in Breisgau: Herder, 1950), 6:401-7, 580-93. For this particular remark, see 587-88.

28. See Kenneth Hein, *Eucharist and Excommunication*, 2d ed. (Bern: H. Lang, 1975).

29. *Rite of Christian Initiation of Adults,* par. 9, pp. 4-5.

30. As cited by Joseph H. Crehan, "Ministerial Priesthood: A Survey of Work Since the Council," *Theological Studies* 32 (1971): 496.

## CHAPTER 3

1. As cited by Albrecht Oepke, *Theological Dictionary of the New Testament*, s.v. *"iamomai."*

2. Ibid.

3. William L. Lane, citing D. Daube, in *Commentary on the Gospel of Mark* (Grand Rapids: Wm. B. Eerdmans, 1973), 105.

4. So Lane, on the basis of the Greek text; see ibid., 106.

5. So Joseph A. Fitzmyer, *The Gospel According to Luke* I–IX (New York: Doubleday & Co., 1981), 592 n. 31; see also 580 for his discussion of the Old Testament background of sin and sickness connections.

6. Origen, *Homily 8* on Leviticus, as cited by Adolf von Harnack, *The Mission and Expansion of Christianity in the First Three Centuries*, Eng. trans. by James Moffatt (Gloucester, Mass.: Peter Smith, 1963), 110 n. 4.

7. *Concilii Tridentini Actorum*, 7: 268.

8. For typical texts, see Paul F. Palmer, ed., *Sacraments and Forgiveness* (Westminster, Md.: Newman Press, 1960), 83, 110.

9. For examples, see ibid., 100, 138, 154.

10. Paul Anciaux, *La Théologie du Sacrement de Pénitence au XII$^e$ siècle* (Louvain: E. Nauwelaerts, 1949), 177, 277. Anciaux notes correctly (p. 279) that the sources of inspiration for these commentators are the remarks of Gregory and Jerome (cited in nn. 8, 9, above) who were reacting against the priestly abuse of this power.

11. For a typical example, see *Concilii Tridentini Actorum*, 7: 301.

12. Catechesis 10, 13, in *The Works of Saint Cyril of Jerusalem*, vol. 61 of *Fathers of the Church*, trans. Leo P. McCauley and Anthony A. Stephenson (Washington, D.C.: Catholic University of America Press, 1969), 204.

13. For examples, see Harnack, *Mission and Expansion*, 109.

14. For this and similar examples, see ibid., 114–16; Vogel, *Le Pécheur et la Pénitence* 95–96; also, Gervais Dumeige, "Médecin (Le Christ)," in *Dictionnaire de la Spiritualité*, vol. 10, c. 891–901.

15. Harnack, *Mission and Expansion*, 108; see also 120–22 for the pastoral implementation.

16. See Rudolph Arbesmann, "The Concept of 'Christus Medicus' in St. Augustine," *Traditio* 10 (1954): 1–28.

17. *In Joh. evang.*, 3.2f., as cited in ibid., 13.

18. *Sermo Guelferb*, 17.1, as cited in ibid., 19.

19. Even in the thirteenth century Bonaventure still uses the *medicus* image in his *Breviloquium*, especially when treating of the sacraments in his chapter on "Sacramental Medicine." *Omnia Opera* (Quaracchi: Collegium St. Bonaventure, 1891), 5: 265–80.

20. Text in Cyrille Vogel, *Le Pécheur et la Pénitence au Moyen-Âge* (Paris: Cerf, 1969), 143–44; emphasis added. See also 65 (Columban).

21. *Concilii Tridentini Actorum*, 6: 262; emphasis added.

22. For example, see ibid., 6: 403.

23. Ibid., 7: 348.

24. Ibid., 7: 311.

25. *Rituale Romanum Pauli Pontificis Maximis* (Paris, 1863), no. 78.

26. The most interesting discussions are to be found in the sessions on the "Use and Abuse of the Sacraments," *Concilii Tridentini Actorum*, 6: 401–7, 580–93.

27. See, for example, Holmes, *Future Shape of Ministry;* idem, *Priest in Community*.

28. See David Tracy, *The Analogical Imagination: Christian Theology and the Culture of Pluralism* (New York: Crossroad, 1981), 71.

29. *Ministry in America*, ed. Strommen, Schuller, and Brekke, 23–53.

30. The remarks that follow in this chapter are indebted to the more extensive study I published as "A Theological Critique of the Professional Model of Ministry," *St. Luke's Journal of Theology* 25 (1982): 86–105.

31. *Concilii Tridentini Actorum*, 6: 587–88.

32. D. T. Hall and Benjamin Schneider, *Organizational Climates and Careers: The Work Lives of Priests* (New York: Seminar Press, 1972).

33. Published as *The Catholic Priest in the United States* in three volumes by United States Catholic Conference, Washington, D.C.: *Historical Investigations* (1971), ed. John T. Ellis; *Psychological Investigations* (1972), ed. Eugene C. Kennedy and Victor J. Heckler; *Sociological Investigations* (1972), ed. Andrew M. Greeley.

34. I have developed this in detail in *Real Presence*.

35. Erik H. Erikson, *Insight and Responsibility* (New York: W. W. Norton, 1964), 30.

36. Charles E. Winquist, *Practical Hermeneutics: A Revised Agenda for the Ministry* (Chico, Calif.: Scholars Press, 1980), 41, 91.

37. C. K. Barrett, *A Commentary on the Second Epistle to the Corinthians* (London: A. & C. Black, 1973), 178.

38. Paul Ricoeur, *The Symbolism of Evil* (New York: Harper & Row, 1967), 353.

39. Bernard Lonergan, *Method in Theology* (New York: Herder & Herder, 1972), 356; emphasis added.

40. Harnack, *Mission and Expansion,* 108.

## CHAPTER 4

1. Lonergan, *Method in Theology,* 355.

2. Ibid., 361–62.

3. Norbert Mette, *Theorie der Praxis* (Düsseldorf: Patmos, 1978), 26. Throughout this section I am particularly indebted to Mette's thorough historical analysis.

4. Ibid., 31–32.

5. Ibid., 36.

6. For a discussion of the functional approach of Graf and others, see ibid., 56–57.

7. Ibid., 65.

8. Matthew Lamb, "The Theory-Praxis Relationship in Contemporary Christian Theologies," *Proceedings of the Catholic Theological Society of America* 31 (1976): 149–78.

9. Ibid., 171–73. Zerfass, for example, has applied a similar model to practical theology; see his "Praktische Theologie," 167ff.

10. For a general discussion of this problem, see Jürgen Habermas, *Communication and the Evolution of Society* (Boston: Beacon Press, 1979).

11. Cyprian, *The Unity of the Catholic Church,* 6, in *Early Latin Theology,* ed. S. L. Greenslade (Philadelphia: Westminster Press, 1956), 127–28.

12. Augustine, *On Baptism, Against the Donatists,* III.14, in *Nicene and Post-Nicene Fathers,* ed. Phillip Schaff (Grand Rapids: Wm. B. Eerdmans, 1979), 4: 439.

13. *Sermo ad Caesariensis ecclesiae plebem,* 2, CSEL 53 (Leipzig: G. Freytag, 1910), 170.

14. Thomas Aquinas retains the same insight: "To perform acts appropriate to the church as she exists in the present, they [Christians] are deputed by a certain spiritual seal imprinted on them which is called character" (*Summa Theologicae,* III, q. 63, I, 2); cf. Blackfriars' edition, *The Sacraments (3a.60–65),* ed. David Bourke (New York: McGraw-Hill, 1975), 77.

15. See Eliseo Ruffini, "Character as a Concrete Visible Element of the Sacrament in Relation to the Church," *The Sacraments in General,* ed. E. Schillebeeckx and B. Willems, Concilium 31 (Paramus, N.J.: Paulist/ Newman Press, 1968), 101–14.

16. Mette, "Praktische Theologie," 199.

17. *Rite of Christian Initiation of Adults,* par. 9, 2, p. 5.

## CHAPTER 5

1. Emmanuel Cardinal Suhard, *Priests Among Men* (Chicago: Fides Publishers, 1949).

2. Ibid., 50.

3. Ch. 1, par. 7, in *Documents,* 21.

4. Introduction, par. 4, in *Documents,* 201–2.

5. Part 1, par. 11, in *Documents,* 209.

6. Ch. 4, par. 44, in *Documents,* 246.

7. M. J. Congar, *Lay People in the Church: A Study for a Theology of Laity,* trans. Donald Attwater, rev. ed. (Westminster, Md.: Newman Press, 1965); idem, *A Gospel Priesthood,* trans. P. J. Hepburne-Scott (New York: Herder & Herder, 1967).

8. Ch. 6, par. 19, in *Documents,* 454.

9. Ibid.

10. Ibid., in *Documents,* 455.

11. See the essays by John T. Ellis, Michael V. Gannon, and David J. O'Brien in *Catholic Priest in United States: Historical Investigations,* ed. Ellis.

12. Frederick Schulze, *Manual of Pastoral Theology* (Milwaukee: N. H. Wiltzius, 1899); William Stang, Pastoral Theology (Cincinnati: Benziger, 1903).

13. James Cardinal Gibbons, *The Ambassadors of Christ* (Baltimore: John Murphy, 1896).

14. Raymond Hostie, *Religion and the Psychology of Jung,* trans. G. R. Lamb (New York: Sheed & Ward, 1957); idem, *Pastoral Counseling,* trans. Gilbert Barth (New York: Sheed & Ward, 1966).

15. André Godin, *The Pastor as Counselor,* trans. Bernard Phillips (New York: Holt, Rinehart & Winston, 1965); idem, *From Religious Experience to a Religious Attitude* (Chicago: Loyola University Press, 1965).

16. John R. Cavanagh, *Fundamental Pastoral Counseling* (Milwaukee: Bruce Publishing, 1963); idem, *Fundamental Marriage Counseling,* rev. ed. (Milwaukee: Bruce Publishing, 1966); Charles A. Curran, *Religious Values in Counseling and Psychotherapy* (New York: Sheed & Ward, 1969); idem, *Psychological Dynamics in Religious Living* (New York: Seabury Press, 1971).

17. George Hagmaier and Robert W. Gleason, *Moral Problems Now* (New York: Sheed & Ward, 1964); Josef Goldbrunner, *Realization: The Anthropology of Pastoral Care* (Notre Dame, Ind.: University of Notre Dame Press, 1966); C. W. Brister, *Pastoral Care in the Church* (New York: Harper & Row, 1964).

18. Nouwen, *Creative Ministry;* idem, *The Wounded Healer: Ministry in Contemporary Society* (Garden City, N.Y.: Doubleday & Co., 1972).

19. See Kennedy and Heckler, eds., *Catholic Priest in United States: Psychological Investigations.*

20. For the initial discussion, see ibid., 10–11.

21. Ibid., 12; cf. Andrew Greeley's remarks on these results in *Priests in the United States: Reflections on a Survey* (Garden City, N.Y.: Doubleday & Co., 1972), 92–93.

22. James D. Whitehead and Evelyn E. Whitehead, *Method in Ministry: Theological Reflection and Christian Ministry* (New York: Seabury Press, 1980).

23. Mette, *Theorie der Praxis,* 325.

24. For his definition of transcendental experience, see Rahner, *Foundations of Christian Faith*, 20.

25. Ira Progoff, *At a Journal Workshop: The Basic Text and Guide for Using the Intensive Journal* (New York: Dialogue House Library, 1975).

26. See above, n. 19.

27. J. Paul Sampley, *Pauline Partnership in Christ: Christian Community and Commitment in Light of Roman Law* (Philadelphia: Fortress Press, 1980), 61.

28. Ibid., 62–70.

29. See Robert Banks, *Paul's Idea of Community: The Early House Churches in the Historical Setting* (Grand Rapids: Wm. B. Eerdmans, 1980), and Käsemann, *Commentary on Romans*, 412–13.

30. See Power's discussion in *Gifts That Differ*.

31. R. M. Kanter, *Commitment and Community: Communes and Utopias in Sociological Perspective* (Cambridge: Harvard University Press, 1972).

32. In *The Unchurched American*, a study conducted by the Princeton Religion Research Center and the Gallup Organization in 1978, the question of meaning does emerge (p. 23), but a careful reading of the questionnaire employed for the study reveals only a limited understanding of shared meaning in religion.

## CHAPTER 6

1. *Rite of Christian Initiation of Adults*, par. 4, p. 1.

2. Ibid., par. 14, p. 3.

3. Ibid., par. 15, p. 4.

4. Ibid., par. 19, n. 4, p. 5.

5. Ibid., par. 81, p. 20.

6. Ibid., par. 152, p. 43.

7. For a discussion of the scrutinies, exorcisms, etc., that give this Lenten preparation its special character, see Kavanagh, *Shape of Baptism*.

8. *Rite of Christian Initiation of Adults*, par. 163, p. 45.

9. Ibid., par. 38, p. 8.

10. Ibid., par. 39, p. 8.

11. Ibid., par. 235, p. 74.

12. The *Rite of Christian Initiation of Adults* makes a distinction between a sponsor and a godparent (see pars. 42, 43, p. 10), even though they may be the same person. In this chapter I am employing the term "sponsor" in a broader sense than that of the *Rite of Christian Initiation of Adults*.

13. For a general description of the Vatican II legislation on the anointing of the sick see R. Kevin Seasoltz, *New Liturgy, New Laws* (Collegeville, Minn.: Liturgical Press, 1980), 67–70.

14. For the historical background see Bernhard Poschmann, *Penance and the Anointing of the Sick* (New York: Herder & Herder, 1964), 234–57; Antoine Chavasse, "Prières pour les malades et onction sacramentelle," in *Introduction à la Liturgie. Eglise en Prière*, ed. Aime-Georges Martimort, 3d ed. (Paris: Desclée, 1965), 596–612.

15. "Dogmatic Constitution" (*Lumen Gentium*) par. 11 in *Documents*, 28.

16. For citations from the text of the ritual, see *The Rites of the Catholic Church as Revised by the Second Vatican Ecumenical Council* (New York: Pueblo Publishing, 1976), par. 1, p. 582.

17. I have developed these ideas more fully in "Symbols of Abundance, Symbols of Need," in *Liturgy and Social Justice*, ed. Mark Searle (Collegeville, Minn.: Liturgical Press, 1980), 72–102.

18. See Paul Ricoeur, "Biblical Hermeneutics," *Semeia* 4 (1975): 127.

19. See *The Rites*, par. 5, p. 583.

20. See Käsemann's remarks on these verses in *Commentary on Romans*, 229–32.

21. *The Rites*, par. 2, p. 582. The reference is to Col. 1:24 and Rom. 8:19–21.

22. *The Rites*, par. 50, p. 595.

23. This remains theologically true even if "to heal" is a textual addition; see I. Howard Marshall, *The Gospel of Luke* (Grand Rapids: Wm. B. Eerdmans, 1978), 352.

24. *The Rites*, par. 42, p. 593; see also, par. 33, p. 590.

25. Ibid., par. 7, p. 584.

26. Ibid.

27. In addition to my *Real Presence*, see my "Formative Experience and Intentional Liturgy," *Studies in Formative Spirituality* 3 (1982): 351–61.

28. *The Rites*, par. 44, p. 593.

29. Ibid., par. 77, p. 603.

30. Ibid., par. 3, p. 582.

31. Ibid., par. 4, pp. 582–83.

32. Erikson, *Insight and Responsibility*, 30.

33. See Alexander Ganoczy, *Theologie der Natur* (Zürich: Benziger, 1982), 38–70.

34. Rahner, *Foundations of Christian Faith*, 78–79.

35. Again, Rahner's comments on the transcendental nature of our experience are penetrating; ibid., 26–39.

36. See B. Holmberg, *Paul and Power: The Structure of Authority in the Primitive Church Reflected in the Pauline Epistles* (Philadelphia: Fortress Press, 1980), 76–77.

37. *St. Francis of Assisi: Writings and Early Biographies*, ed. Marion A. Habig et al. (Chicago: Franciscan Herald Press, 1973), 130–31.

38. *The Rites*, par. 5, p. 583.

39. Ibid., pars. 25, 76, pp. 587, 603, as well as penitential rites before the communion of the sick; par. 52, p. 595.

40. "The Church Today" (*Gaudium et Spes*), par. 7, in *Documents*, 205.

41. See Vatican II's "Decree on Apostolate of Laity," par. 12 in *Documents*, 503.

42. At the insistence of many bishops at Vatican II, earlier drafts about youth in the church were replaced by the stronger statements of the accepted documents; see *Documents*, 503–4 n. 38.

43. See, for example, "Decree on Bishops' Pastoral Office," par. 30 n. 2, in *Documents,* 419.

44. "Decree on Apostolate of Laity," par. 12, in *Documents,* 504.

45. Vatican II clearly reiterated the connection between the sacraments of initiation (baptism, confirmation, Eucharist) and the witness and mission of all Christians; see ibid., par. 3, in *Documents,* 492.

46. Ibid., par. 12, in *Documents,* 504.

47. E. Erikson, *Dimensions of a New Identity: Jefferson Lectures 1973* (New York: W. W. Norton, 1974), 72.

48. Ibid., 27.

49. For some typical references, see Erikson, *Insight and Responsibility,* 124–30; idem, *Identity: Youth and Crisis* (New York: W. W. Norton, 1968), 128–35.

50. *Insight and Responsibility,* 125.

51. See James Fowler, *Stages of Faith: The Psychology of Human Development and the Quest for Meaning* (New York: Harper & Row, 1981), 109–10; idem, "Faith and the Structuring of Meaning," in *Toward Moral and Religious Maturity* (Morristown, N.J.: Silver Burdett, 1980), 51–85, especially 71–72. Fowler acknowledges that some adults never arrive at this stage, others do so only in their thirties or forties.

52. *"Dogmatic Constitution on Revelation" (Dei Verbum),* par. 5, in *Documents,* 113.

53. Fowler reminds us that each stage is a value, not an achievement; see his "Faith and Structuring of Meaning," 82.

54. *Insight and Responsibility,* 90–91.

55. Erikson's remarks on ritualization and identity of youth are helpful here; see his *Toys and Reasons: Stages in the Ritualization of Experience* (New York: W. W. Norton, 1977), 109–10.

56. E. Erikson, *Childhood and Society,* rev. ed. (New York: W. W. Norton, 1964), 263.

57. *De carnis resurrectione,* 8, in *Enchiridion Patristicum,* ed. M. J. Rouët (Freiburg: Herder, 1919), 181 (my translation).

58. Richard McBrien, *Catholicism,* 2 vols. (Minneapolis: Winston Press, 1980), 2: 1147–50.

59. See Don Browning, *Generative Man: Psychoanalytic Perspectives* (Philadelphia: Westminster Press, 1973), 162–78.

60. Henri de Motherlant, *La Ville dont le prince est un enfant* (Paris: Gallimard, 1967), 175. The play was actually written in 1951.

61. "The Church Today," par. 66, in *Documents,* 275.

62. D. Levinson, et al., *The Seasons of a Man's Life* (New York: Alfred A. Knopf, 1978), 335.

63. Erikson, *Insight and Responsibility,* 133.

64. Suzanne Reichard, Florine Livson, and Paul G. Peterson, *Aging and Personality* (New York: John Wiley & Sons, 1962), 170–71.

65. Erikson, *Childhood and Society,* 269.

66. See David O. Moberg, "Religiosity in Old Age," in *Middle Age and Aging*, ed. Bernice L. Neugarten (Chicago: University of Chicago Press, 1968), 497–508.

67. Interesting in this respect is Paul's linking of "why many among you are sick and infirm" (1 Cor. 11:30) with eucharistic participation; see Hans Conzelmann, *First Corinthians*, ed. G. W. Macrae, Eng. trans. J. W. Leitch (Philadelphia: Fortress Press, 1975), 203.

68. See above, n. 32.

69. Thomas of Celano, *First Life of St. Francis*, VI, in *St. Francis of Assisi*, ed. Habig, et al., 318.